MANIPUR
Geography and Regional Development

MANIPUR
Geography and Regional Development

Vedaja Sanjenbam

RAJESH PUBLICATIONS
New Delhi - 110 002

MANIPUR

Geography and Regional Development

ISBN : 978-81-85891-19-4 (P.B.)
ISBN : 978-93-83684-35-9 (H.B.)

Published by :
Sanjay Gupta
RAJESH PUBLICATIONS
1, Ansari Road, Darya Ganj,
New Delhi - 110 002
Ph.: 011-23274550

Typesetting by :
Sanjay Gupta
New Delhi- 110 002

Printed in India at :
Vijeta Offset Printers, Delhi-2

Ist Published in India : 1998
Second Edition : 2009
Third Edition : 2017

Preface

Integrated regional development aims not only at integrating social and economic activities which influence the life of the people but also at optimal location of investments as necessary input to reduce the gap between the developed and developing regions. Our Five Year Plans of economic development have emphasized the need for the location of specific area plans for an integrated and balanced development of the country with major thrusts on enhanced agricultural productivity, creation of employment opportunities and provision for essential facilities and amenities for the people, particularly the poorer section of the society living in the countryside. Resource appraisal and identification of growth centres are, therefore, considered essential steps in the formulation of regional development plans.

The present exercise is an attempt towards the formulation of an integrated regional development plan for Manipur based on growth centre approach as growth concentration results in economies of scale and the development as a process of innovation and growth does not occur everywhere at the same time but originates only at certain points from where it percolates to other centres.

To transform the space economy of the state, central places of various magnitude have been identified and their hinterlands, forming the levels of planning regions, delineated in the study. Perspective planning for a period of 10 years have been presented in the sectoral and spatial frames to mitigate the disparities in development of the valley and hill regions of Manipur in the study.

It is a great pleasure to express my sincere gratitude to Professor R. P. Singh, Head, Department of Geography, Manipur

University for his valuable suggestions, advice and guidance, and to Professor B. N. Sinha and Professor R. N. P. Sinha, ex-Visiting Professors in the Department of Geography, Manipur University , late R.K. Birendra Singh, Secretary, Manipur Legislative Assembly and Shri A.S. Arthur, Minister of Forest and Environment, Government of Manipur for their valuable suggestions and encouragement.

I express my sincere thanks to the authorities of the Directorate of Census Operations, Manipur for the Census data; Department of Economics and Statistics, Government of Manipur for the statistical profile; and Directorate of Planning, Govt. of Manipur for information about the Five Year Plans and development profile of the state. I also acknowledge the help of the officials of the Directorate of Industry, Agriculture, Veterinary and Animal Husbandry, Education, Medical and Health Services, Town Planning and other development departments of the State Government for their cooperation and help in providing me the required information, data and official reports, which immensely helped me in my study.

I gladly acknowledge my indebtedness to the authors of various books and articles listed in the Bibliography whose learned works have helped me in completing this study.

The constant help, encouragement and inspiration of my father - Sanjenbam Vedajit Singh and assistance of my younger sister-Sanjenbam Visheswari have been exceedingly helpful to me in giving this work its present shape. I express my sincere gratitude and thanks to them.

Vedaja Sanjenbam

Khwairakpam Leikai
Sega Road
Imphal - 795001

Preface to the Second Edition

The first edition of Manipur : Geography and Regional Development went out of print within a year. The overwhelming interest of the students of geography and general readers in this modest publication necessitated its second edition within a short span of less than two years. The comments and concerns of the academic community have been given due consideration in the present edition of the book.

Most of the tables, maps and text of the book have been updated, modified and analysed to suit the need and requirements of the students, planners and general readers. Some new maps and tables have been incorporated in the book to make it more informative and useful.

I am extremely thankful to the authorities of the various departments of the state government for their help in updating the information given in the book.

I express my sincere gratitude and thanks to my father Sanjenbam Vedajit Singh for his constant help in updating this book.

Imphal **Vedaja Sanjenbam**
15th August, 2000

Contents

List of Maps and Diagrams

List of Tables

1

Introduction

1.1 Statement of the Problem

Planning in India is largely concerned with the balanced development of areas and people. As such, since its inception, planning has been dynamic in its approach to develop regions and achieve social justice for the people. About five decades of planned development has resulted in unequal development of regions and growing social tensions. As a remedial measure to this phenomenon, problem regions such as backward areas, hill areas, drought prone areas and flood affected areas were given special consideration in the successive Five Year Plans. Despite special plans and budgets, the problems faced by these regions remained partially unsolved. The recent trend observed therein is the faster rate of outward mobility of manpower and resources from these regions. Siphoning of natural resources, on the one hand, and of active working population, on the other, augments poverty and cements backwardness in these areas. Leakage of natural resources from the backward regions of the country leaves limited scope behind for regional development. It is in this context that a study relating to assessment of the role of various plans and their implementation becomes imperative and important.

Manipur (Area 22,327 km^2/Population 18,37,149 in 1991), a small backward hill state in North East India, can broadly be divided into three natural regions-the Manipur hills, the Manipur valley and the Barak basin (Fig. 1.1). The Manipur hills provide the geographic base to the state as they cover about 90 per cent of

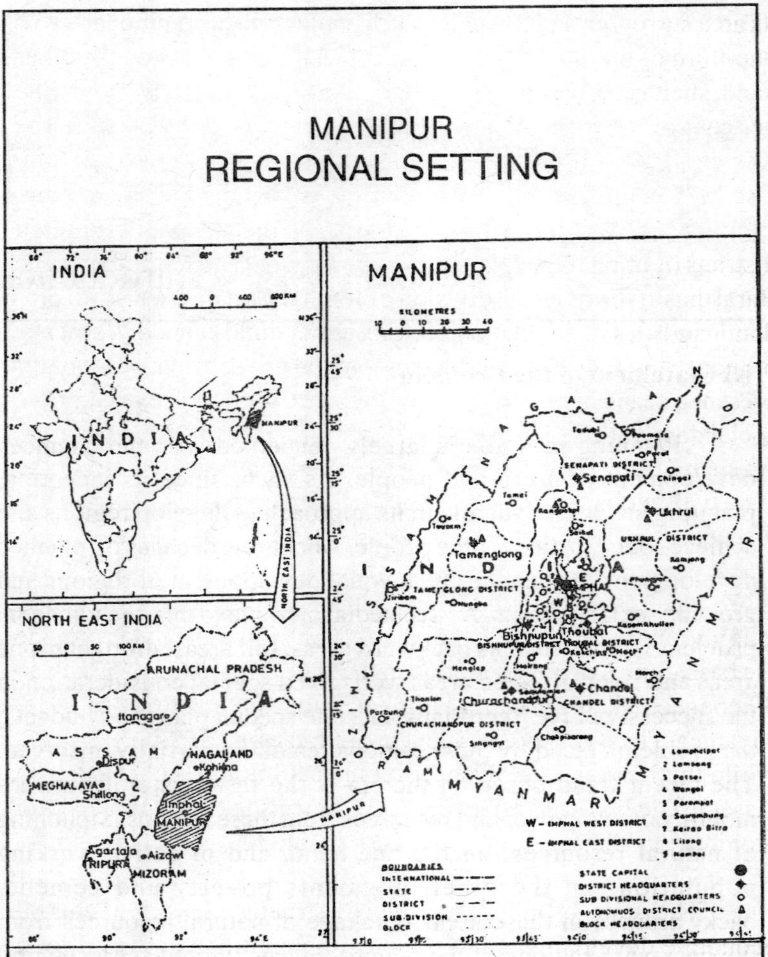
MANIPUR
REGIONAL SETTING
INDIA
INDIA
MANIPUR
NORTH EAST INDIA
NORTH EAST INDIA
ARUNACHAL PRADESH
INDIA
Itanagar
ASSAM
Dispur
NAGALAND
Kohima
MEGHALAYA
Shillong
Imphal
MANIPUR
Agartala
TRIPURA
Aizawl
MIZORAM
MANIPUR
MANIPUR
KILOMETRES
NAGALAND
ASSAM
MIZORAM
MYANMAR
MYANMAR
INDIA
Senapati
SENAPATI DISTRICT
Ukhrul
UKHRUL DISTRICT
Tamenglong
TAMENGLONG DISTRICT
Bishnupur
BISHNUPUR DISTRICT
Thoubal
THOUBAL DISTRICT
Chandel
CHANDEL DISTRICT
Churachandpur
CHURACHANDPUR DISTRICT
W - IMPHAL WEST DISTRICT
E - IMPHAL EAST DISTRICT
BOUNDARIES
INTERNATIONAL
STATE
DISTRICT
SUB-DIVISION
BLOCK
STATE CAPITAL
DISTRICT HEADQUARTERS
SUB DIVISIONAL HEADQUARTERS
AUTONOMOUS DISTRICT COUNCIL
BLOCK HEADQUARTERS

Fig. 1.1

its area surrounding the small central valley and accommodate over one-third of the state population. The Manipur valley, on the other hand, shelters about two-thirds of the state population in about nine per cent of the area. The tiny Barak basin, a riverine plain on the western border of the state, has a moderate density of population. The hills comprise five tribal districts of Senapati, Tamenglong, Churachandpur, Chandel and Ukhrul ; and the valley of four plain districts of Imphal East, Imphal West, Thoubal and Bishnupur. The Barak basin forms a sub-division of Imphal East district. With predominantly tribal population, shifting agricultural economy, absence of industries and least of urbanization, the hill districts of Manipur present a scene of poverty, unemployment, economic exploitation, social deprivation, poor health, illiteracy and lack of infrastructure. As such, it is difficult to think of the balanced development of the state without improving the lot of the tribal people living in the hill districts.

Manipur does not have any water transport system. Recently it has been provided with a nominal railway link. The roads provide the basic routes of transportation in the state. The National Highway 39 connects the state capital Imphal with Moreh, a town on Indo-Myanmar (Burma) border, and Dimapur, the rail head in Nagaland, while the National Highway 53 connects Imphal with Silchar in Assam. The National Highway 150 connects the state capital with Kohima via Ukhrul and Aizawl via Tipaimukh.

The state by its topographical structure had problems of economic development and socio-economic transformation for a pretty long period. Manipur presents a true picture of the conditions prevailing in the scarcity pockets of the Indian economy. The low per capita income, a fast increasing population, absence of industries, huge but mostly unskilled manpower are the familiar contours of this economically backward and depressed region (Singh, 1982). The economic stagnation of the state has led a large proportion of her people, around 45 per cent, to live a life below the poverty line.

The strategic location of the state in a sensitive region adjoining the international boundary, the inequality of the living standards of the valley and hill people, the lack of employment opportunities, meagre transport facilities, all emphasise the need for a programme for the balanced and integrated development of the state on a scale and pattern adequate for the purpose.

1.2 Conceptual Framework

The concept of integrated regional development in its true scientific meaning refers to two types of integration-functional and spatial, which are themselves interrelated. Functional integration refers to the integration of all social and economic activities like health, education, agriculture, industries, transport, etc., which influence the life of people and often overlap. A change in one sector almost invariably brings about the corresponding change in another. The community development programme in India tried to achieve functional integration by establishing an integrated staffing pattern. Specialists from different government departments representing health, education, agriculture, industry, etc. were brought together as a team at the block level and it was expected that daily interaction among them will also lead to an integrated development of the rural areas. However, this has not happened.

The spatial relationship among various socio-economic activities depend a great deal on where they are located. It is seen that activities often cluster in hierarchical pattern in space. Their location depends on factors like level of development, demand for specific functions and their supply, their accessibility in terms of roads and transportation, time and distance of travel, level of income of the people, cost of these functions, etc. Large portions of our rural areas are deprived of many basic amenities, while there are areas with concentration of such functions.

Integrated regional development, thus, refers to the appropriate location of social and economic activities over a physical space for the balanced development of a region. The idea of an appropriate location is by definition selective. In other words, each and every settlement cannot have all kinds of functions. It has been observed by location theorists that there is a hierarchy of settlements based on the number of functions of different orders and specialisation, and also on the basis of the area served by a settlement. All functions of different orders, therefore, need to be located in the most appropriate places selected on the basis of their hierarchy and centrality.

Integrated regional development is also concerned with the development of backward areas. If the existing hierarchy of settlements in a particular region is utilised for formulating a development plan, then areas far away from the important centres of economic activity may remain permanently underdeveloped. Some inducement for growth is, therefore, necessary in backward areas in the form of overheads and infrastructures in decentralised but selective locations.

Integrated regional development is, thus, based on the principles of 'selectivity' on the one hand, and 'decentralisation' on the other. It suggests a framework for decentralising economic and social activities by locating specific functions in appropriate places. The network, thus created, provides a meaningful infrastructure which can attract and sustain a diversified and growing economy. The central place system and growth centre approach provide the most suitable methodology for a balanced policy between selectivity and decentralisation of economic activities for the integrated development of the state.

Thus, the integrated regional development programme is a multi-level, multi-sector and multi-section concept. Obviously, it encompasses development of a region (i) at various levels in spatial hierarchy, such as viable cluster of villages, block and district, (ii) at various sectors/sub-sectors of economy, such as agriculutre, industry, transport, education and health, etc., and (iii) at various poorer sections/sub-sections of population, such as landless labourers, artisans, small and marginal farmers, scheduled castes and scheduled tribes, etc. From an operational viewpoint, integrated regional development plan has got the thrust in the framework of block-level planning. But it should not be taken as an isolated exercise, instead it is to be fitted into a hierarchy of levels, both above and below.

1.3 Objectives of the Study

The objectives of the study are as follows :

i. To make an appraisal of areal resources of the state in view of their availability, mode of utilisation, potentiality and prospects for their development;

ii. To identify and rank growth centres and central places of various orders and delineate their tributary areas or complementary zones;

iii. To prepare a plan based on growth centres for an integrated regional development of the state; and

iv. To identify the development schemes of local importance to benefit the society in general and the poor in particular.

1.4 Review of Literature

Integrated regional development planning relates to the integrated development of various sectors of economy of a region, particularly a small state or an ecological region, as a unit of planning. Under the Five Year Plans efforts have been made to remove the regional disparities in economic development. The Ford Foundation and the National Institute of Rural Development (NIRD), Hyderabad have made concerted efforts in formulating plans for regional development by taking district, sub-division and block as units of planning. Different ecological zones and socio-economic settings were selected by the NIRD for choosing such areas. Later on, various other institutions, both private and public, utilised the concepts of regional development planning and growth centres for formulating plans at regional, district and block levels. The purpose was mainly to develop a methodology for preparing area development plans.

The publication of *Planning Rural Growth Centres for Integrated Area Development : A Study in Miryalguda Taluka* by Lalit K. Sen *et al.* in 1971 marked the beginning of regional development studies in India. A host of similar studies were subsequently taken up by the NIRD, which include *Regional Planning for Social Facilities-An Examination of Central Place Concepts and Their Application : A Case Study of Eastern Maharashtra* by Sudhir Wanmali (1973), *Growth Centres in Raichur-An Integrated Area Development Plan for a District in Karnataka* by Lalit K. Sen *et al.* (1975), *Integrated Area Development Plan for West District, Manipur* by Wahiduddin Khan and K.S. Ramesh (1976), *Plan for Integrated Rural Development in Pauri Garhwal* by Wahiduddin Khan and R.N. Tripathy (1976), *Block Plan in the District Frame : A Development Plan for Madakasira Block in Anantapur District, Andhra Pradesh* by R.N. Tripathy *et al.* (1980), *Planning for Integrated Rural Development Programme : Amalapuram Block* by R.N. Tripathy, B.K. Thapliyal and F.M. Pradhan (1981), etc. The Indian Council of Social Science Research (ICSSR), New Delhi and the University Grants Commission (UGC) also sponsored a number of studies in the field of integrated regional development planning, such as *Micro-level Planning : A Case Study of Karnal Area, Haryana, India* by L.S. Bhat *et al.* (1976) and *Central Places and Spatial Organisation in a Backward Economy : Gorakhpur Region-A Study in Integrated Regional Development* by Jagdish Singh (1979), which mark a pattern of development studies in the regional setting. *Block Level Planning with Focus on Employment Generation* by Girish K. Misra *et al.* (1987), *Strategy for Integrated Area Development : Case Study of North Kanara District (Karnataka)* by L.S. Bhat (1988) and *Integrated Area Development and Planning* by Surendra Singh (1990) are similar studies at the micro-level in which sophisticated tools and techniques have been utilised for developmental planning.

At the state level very few studies have so far been taken up for analysing the socio-economic parameters of development in Manipur. Besides *Statistical Account of the Native State of Manipur and the Hill Territory under its Rule* by R. Brown (1873), the *Gazetteer of Manipur* by E.W. Dun (1886), *Techno-Economic Survey of Manipur* formulated by the National Council of Applied Economic Research (1961) and *Geography of Manipur* by R.P. Singh (1982), there are only the census publications and mimeographed reports of various departments of the state government, which throw light on the development perspectives of the state as a whole. Spatial Planning in Chandel District, Manipur by R.P. Singh (1985) and Micro-level Planning :A Case Study of Bishnupur District, Manipur by H. Gitabali Devi (1990) deal with the planning requirements at the district level in two ecological zones-hills and valley, of the state, while the micro-level planning profile of the third ecological zone-the Barak basin, has been portrayed in Rural Development and Micro-Level Planning : A Case Study of Jiribam Block, Manipur by R.P. Singh and Vedaja Sanjenbam (1991).

A large number of regional, rural and tribal development studies have been undertaken by various scholars, institutions and organisations since the Fourth Five Year Plan aiming at the alleviation of poverty of the rural and tribal poor living in the vast inhospitable terrain of the country. In the backdrop of the studies done so far, the present exercise is a modest attempt to formulate an integrated regional development plan for the state of Manipur following the central place concept and growth centre approach.

1.5 Methodology

The model used in this study for preparing an integrated regional development plan for the state of Manipur is based on growth centre concept modelled very closely on the postulates of the central place theory. Growth centres are central places which serve a hinterland consisting of a number of villages. They provide optimal locations for selective investments in agricultural and industrial infra-structure, and social facilities which can be used by the hinterland population.

1.5.1 Central Place Theory

The central place theory was propounded by Walter Christaller (1933), a German geographer and later developed by August Losch (1954) and others. The central place theory consists of the following postulates :

(i) A central place (usually a city, a town or a large village depending on the specific area or region under study), which provides functions and services to its tributary area, is located at the centre of minimum aggregate travel providing minimum cost to the customers and maximum profit to the sellers.

(ii) There is a hierarchy of such central places. The higher order places provide more specialised functions which lower order places do not have. Besides, the higher order places also provide functions normally found in the lower order places.

(iii) The higher order places are fewer in number and more widely spaced than the lower order places. With wide range of functions they have a higher degree of centrality and command a larger tributary area than the lower order places.

(iv) In the hierarchy of central places, each order of place 'nesting' the next lower order places forms a hexagonal tributary area. The 'nesting pattern' or latticing of lower order places within such a command area is, by and large, determined by three principles : (a) marketing, (b) traffic, and (c) administrative. In the market optimising principle, there are two central places of the next lower order for each central place of immediate higher order (K=3), while there are three central places of next lower order for each central place of immediate higher order (K=4) in the traffic optimising principle. There are six central places of next lower order for each central place of immediate higher order (K=7), if the principle of optimum administration predominates (Fig.1.2).

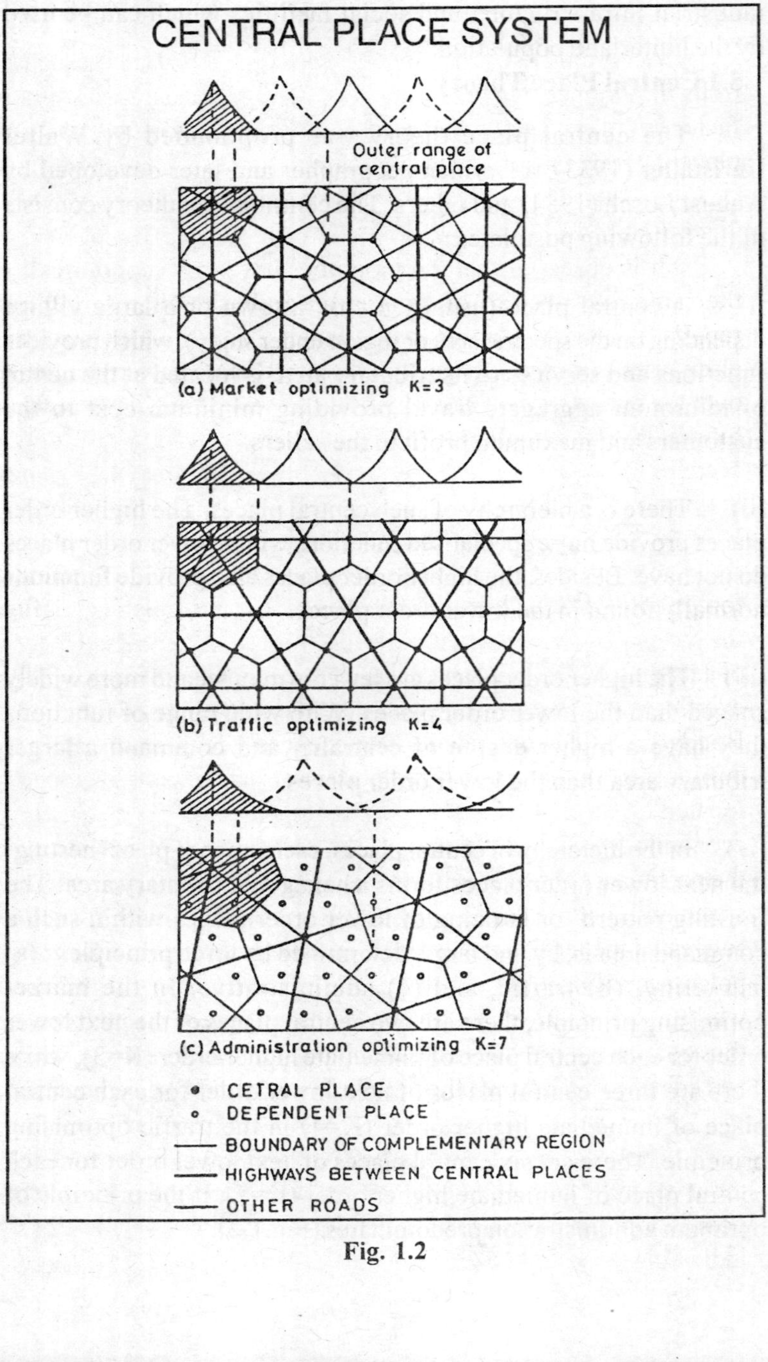
CENTRAL PLACE SYSTEM
Outer range of central place
(a) Market optimizing K=3
(b) Traffic optimizing K=4
(c) Administration optimizing K=7
CETRAL PLACE
DEPENDENT PLACE
BOUNDARY OF COMPLEMENTARY REGION
HIGHWAYS BETWEEN CENTRAL PLACES
OTHER ROADS

Fig. 1.2

According to Christaller, the centrality of a place is a measure of its importance. He recognises population size as an associative factor but places major emphasis on the functional importance of a place in terms of the nature and the range of services offered.

1.5.2 Growth Centre Concept

It is observed that a region does not grow economically at the same rate over all of its area but rather tends to grow most rapidly at a point or points while lagging or remaining stangnant elsewhere. These rapidly growing points (or poles) exert dominance over the entire region. The growth pole theory, originally put forth by the French economist Francois Perroux (1955) attempts to account for the reasons why growth is geographically imbalanced in this way.

Perroux conceived an abstract economic space as field of forces consisting of centres, poles or foci, from which centrifugal forces emanate and to which centripetal forces are attracted in terms of a leading or key industry characterised by high propulsive power, exerting considerable influence through inter-industry linkages. J.R. Boudville (1966) extended the concept to geographical space by defining a regional growth pole as a set of expanding industries located in an urban area and inducing further development of economic activity throughout its zone of influence. In order to avoid the persistent confusion between 'growth pole' related to economic space and that related to geographic space, D.F. Darwent (1969) suggested the term 'growth centre' to denote the latter. The growth poles, according to A. Kuklinski (1972), have national significance while growth centres have just a regional character. Growth centres, thus conceived, provide necessary inputs for maximising economic and social benefits to all the people living within their hinterlands.

There can be several ranks of growth centres depending on their centrality, their degree of functional complexity or their population size. Planners have used several nomenclatures for indicating these ranks (Sen *et al*, 1971; Misra, 1974). The difference between one rank and the next higher or lower one is obvious. Each higher category provides more specialised services than the lower one. Thus, the growth centre concept closely follows the postulates of the central place theory.

1.5.3 Data Collection and Processing

Both primary and secondary data were collected during the period 1991-93 to work out a comprehensive resource inventory of the growth centres and their complementary zones to assess the pattern of resource utilisation and remedies encountering the constraints of resource development processes. While the data about demographic variables including aspects of total, rural and urban population, workers and their categories, marginal workers and non-workers, literate, scheduled caste and scheduled tribe population were collected from the Directorate of Census Operations, Manipur, the data regarding the economic development including agriculture, livestock, fisheries, urban-industrial and public services; assessment of assets and liabilities including land use, land holdings, pattern of cropping, livestock wealth and industrial pursuits; and assessment of various schemes of planning and gaps in planning including aspects of agricultural, industrial, manpower, educational and infrastructural planning have been collected from the concerned departments of the State Government.

The secondary data were also collected from the reports of the block, district and state level development authorities. The annual plans and Five Year Plans of the state, statistical handbooks, Economic Reviews and Tribal Bench Mark Survey reports have been utilised for gathering socio-economic data.

The data collected from the field surveys and secondary sources were tabulated and mapped, and analysed with the help of appropriate statistical techniques and cartographic methods.

1.6 Research Design

The entire study has been divided into five chapters. The

First Chapter, including this section, deals with the conceptual framework, objectives of the study, review of literature, methodology and significance of the work. Chapter Two presents a geographical profile of the state of Manipur, interpreting its physical, economic and cultural characteristics in the regional setting. Methods of identification of the growth centres, demarcation of planning regions and their resource bases, and levels of development have been portrayed in the Third Chapter. Chapter Four reviews the process and performance of the Five Year Plans and presents an integrated approach to the developmental planning of the state in sectoral and spatial frames. The study concludes with Chapter Five summarising the observations and major findings.

1.7 Significance of the Study

The regional development studies have their own relevance to offer experiences and potentials for planning under different geographic and socio-economic conditions. Manipur, with its rich natural resources and high man-land ratio, continues to remain a backward and economically depressed region. The study of backwardness and the role of planning agencies in its eradication, aimed at herein, will be useful in the identification of issues augmenting backwardness and providing suggestions for the balanced development of the state.

2

Geographical Profile

Manipur (Fig. 2.1), a small hilly state in North-East India along the Indo-Myanmar (Burma) border, forms a functional region with Imphal city, the state capital as its nodal centre. It is defined primarily on the basis of bus traffic operating from Imphal. Bus services, being the universal means of public transport, closely reflect the actual pattern of functional interaction and orientation with respect to the nodal centre. Imphal, a flower on the lofty heights (Evans and Brett-James, 1960), is the principal cultural, commercial and political focus of the region, from which the state extends its influence in comparatively less accessible hill areas. The city, as such, emanates growth impetus to the entire state and provides it the regional identity.

Manipur (23°50' N-25°41'N/93°2'E-94°47'E) is centrally located on the eastern arm of the Himalaya-the Purvachal (Chatterjee, 1965), which separates India from Myanmar. The state is almost rectangular in shape with a fertile alluvial plain in the centre surrounded by hill ranges on all sides. It is bounded by Nagaland on the north, Assam on the west, Mizoram on the south-west and Myanmar on the east and south-east with effective physical and administrative-functional barriers.

With an area of 22, 327 km^2 and a population of 18,37, 149 (1991), the state ranks 20th, both in area and population, among the states and union territories in the country. Politico-administratively Manipur comprises nine districts, five in the hills and four in the central valley, which have been divided into 38 subdivisions and 39 commumity/tribal development blocks. The hill districts have been provided with autonomous district councils to administer the social and developmental affairs of the districts. The Zilla Parishads, on the other hand, look after the development activities in the valley districts. Table 2.1 presents the politico-administrative structure of Manipur.

The demographic contrast between the valley and hill districts is reflective of the wide difference in their levels of social and economic development. While the valley is fertile and relatively prosperous, the hills are economically backward and lack even in basic social facilities. As such, there is need for greater economic integration between the valley and hill areas of the state.

2.1 Physical Features

Structurally, the region forms the central segment of the Tertiary foldings on the eastern ramparts of the country. The hill ranges of Manipur and the enclosed intermont basin-the Manipur valley, belong to the Alpine system and the Barak basin, on the western margin, to the sedimentary cover. The state, as such, falls into three landform divisions-the Manipur hills, the Manipur valley and the Barak basin, which differ to much extent in their physical characteristics.

2.1.1 Geology

The rock formations occurring in the state (Fig. 2.1) reveal the geological history to some extent. The Ukhrul limestones, found in a small narrow belt in the northeastern part were formed during the Cretaceous period, about 80 to 90 million years ago, where limestone occurs as lenses in a sequence of gritty sandstone and buff to grey coloured shale. The Disang Group, spread over the eastern half of the state, was deposited in the middle and lower Eocene period. It consists of a monotonous sequence of dark grey shales with thin mudstone, siltstone and sandstone towards the west,

Table 2.1
Manipur : Politico-Administrative Structure

District	Area (km^2)	Population	Number of				
			Subdivisions	CD/TD Blocks	Zilla Parishads/ Auto.Dist. Councils	Villages inhabited	Towns
Imphal East	673	330460	4	4	1	206	3
Imphal West	555	380801	4	4	1	117	10
Thoubal	514	293958	3	3	1	87	9
Bishnupur	496	180773	3	3	1	45	7
Senapati	3271	208406	6	6	2	516	-
Tamenglong	4391	86278	4	4	1	193	-
Churachandpur	4570	176184	5	6	1	504	1
Chandel	3313	71014	4	4	1	292	1
Ukhrul	4544	109275	5	5	1	222	-
Manipur	22327	1837149	38	39	10	2182	31

Source : Census of India 1991.

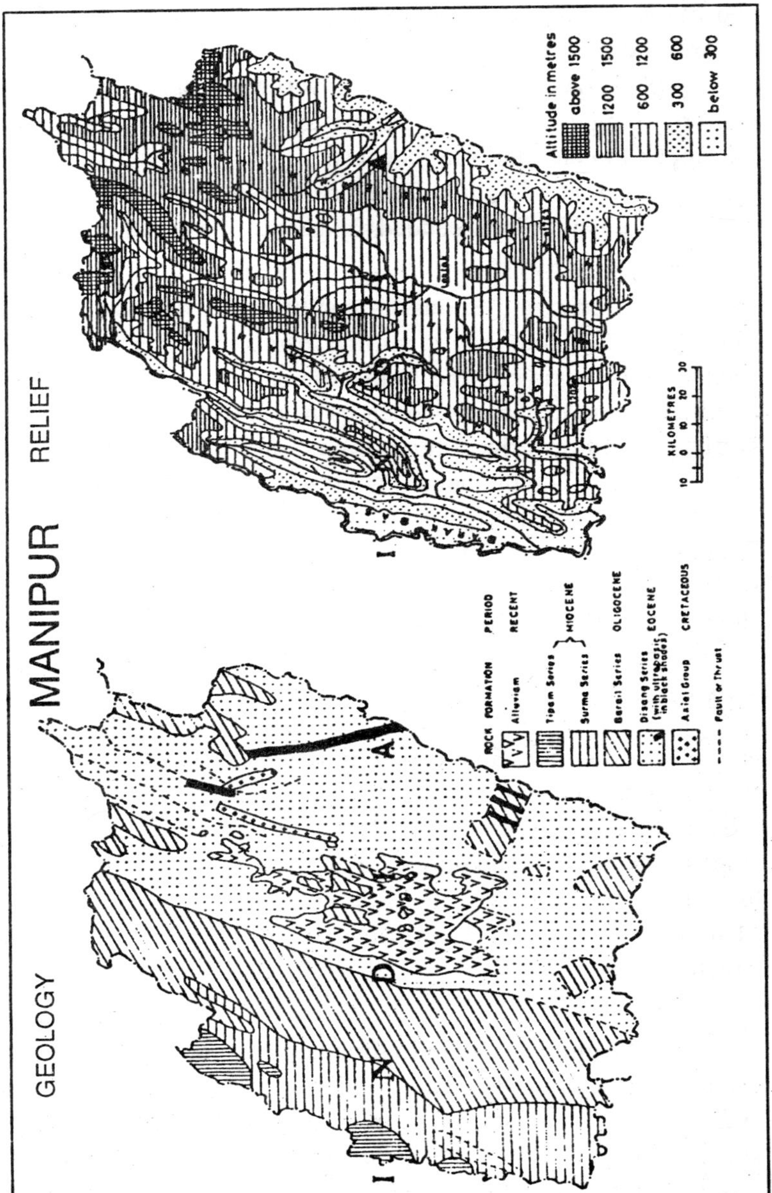
MANIPUR
GEOLOGY
RELIEF
ROCK FORMATION
PERIOD
Alluvium
RECENT
Tipam Series
Surma Series
MIOCENE
Barail Series
OLIGOCENE
Disang Series (with ultrabasics in black shades)
EOCENE
Axial Group
CRETACEOUS
Fault or Thrust
Altitude in metres
above 1500
1200 1500
600 1200
300 600
below 300
KILOMETRES
10 0 10 20 30

Fig. 2.1

and of sandstone, buff-coloured shales and siliceous limestone towards the east.

The Barail Group of rocks, covering the major portion of western Manipur, were formed some 25 to 40 million years ago in the upper Eocene and Oligocene periods. With abundance of carbonaceous materials, it is of considerable economic importance. It consists mostly of well-bedded sandstones, clays and shales.

The Tipam and Surma groups of rocks, deposited in the Miocene period about 18 to 25 million years back, cover the western flanks of the region in the Barak drainage area. Representing argillaceous and arenaceous sequences in their formation, these rocks contain sandy shales, sandstones, mudstones, clay and conglomerates. The Imphal Alluviums, deposited in the Manipur valley, are of recent origin formed within the last 10,000 years. These alluviums, with a thickness of 200 to 300 metres over the underlying Disang shales, contain clay, sand, sandy clay, silt and shingle.

2.1.2 Relief

The Manipur hills consist of a series of parallel ranges extending between the Naga hills in the north and Mizo and Chin hills in the south. These hills, trending north-east to south-west, slope towards south and dominate the regional landscape. These hills broadly fall into two groups-the Manipur eastern hills and the Manipur western hills, which differ to much extent in their layout, structure and relief.

The Manipur eastern hills, forming a compact and continuous chain along the Indo-Myanmar frontier for about 200 km, attain an average height of about 1500 metres. Their breadth ranges from 50 km in the north to about 30 km in the south. The Nupitel, (Mapithel), Chingai, Malain, Angoching and Yomadung are the main ranges of these hills, and Khayangbung (2833 m), Siroi (2568 m) and

Kachubung (2498 m) the important peaks. Formed of the Disang shales, Ukhrul limestones and the serpentinites, the Manipur eastern hills contain a number of important minerals like limestone, chromite, talc, nickel and copper ores.

Spread over the entire western part, the Manipur western hills comprise parallel ridges and valleys running north to south for about 180 km with a breadth of 50 km in the north and 70 km in the south. A number of parallel ranges-Uningthou, Koubru, Khoupum, Nungba, Kalanag, Nungjiabong and Haobi form this wide belt of hills, which are higher in the north and west and lower towards south. Tenipu (2994 m), Koubru (2652 m), Leikot (2831 m), Tamphaba (2664 m) and Iso (2460 m) are important peaks of this area. These hills are composed of the compact sandstones, shales and clays of the Barail series, but their western slopes are covered with sandstones, shales, mudstones and conglomerates of the Surma series.

The Manipur valley, enclosed by Manipur eastern and western hills, is a large intermont basin about 70 km long and 35 km broad having an area of 2067 km^2. It is one of the Himalayan midlands like the Vale of Kashmir and the Kathmandu valley. The valley is a high level flood plain with an elevation of about 760 metres above the mean sea level. The 900 m contour forms its outer limits. It is a lacustrine plain-site of an ancient lake, which was subsequently filled up and uplifted to its present position, the remnant of which occupies the south-east corner of the valley, the Loktak lake (Singh, 1982). The basin presents a flatland topography formed by the alluvial deposits after the Tertiary period. A number of occasional hills and mounds rise above the flat surface which include the Langol, Heingang, Nongmaijing Ching, Langthabal and Waithou etc. Besides, a series of islands project above the water surface of the Loktak lake-Sendra, Ithing, Thanga and Karang being the most important among them.

The Barak basin on the western flanks of the state,beyond the Manipur western hills, is a small plain formed by the headward erosion and subsequent deposition of river Barak and its tributary Jiri. Dotted with low sandstone hillocks, the Barak basin contains rocks of both Surma and Tipam series.

Altitudinal variations, thus, range from 95 m in the Barak basin to 2994 m in the northern hill section of the region. About 27.37 per cent of the total geographical area falls under the altitudinal range of above 1200 m and 53.47 per cent between 600-1200 m. About 12.49 per cent of the area is in the relief range of 300-600 m, 1.38 per cent between 150-300 m, and the rest 5.29 per cent below 150 m (Fig. 2.1).

2.1.3 Drainage

The state is drained by various streams which belong to three river systems (Fig. 2.2). River Manipur and its tributaries-Imphal, Iril, Thoubal, Nambul, Nambol, Khuga and Sekmai with Loktak and other associated lakes form the water resources of the central valley having a catchment of 6332 km^2 forming 28.4 per cent area of the region. These rivers carry a good amount of silt, which has raised their beds considerably. Discharging maximum quantity of water during the monsoon months, they frequently inundate the land along their banks.

River Barak and its tributaries-Irang, Maku, Tuivai, Jiri and their associated streams, which drain the northern and western hill areas, have a catchment of 9042 km^2, about 40.5 per cent area of the entire region. These rivers have long rocky pools, where even in the dry season water remains 10-13 metres deep, alternated with stretches of shingle accompanied by a shallow trickle of water. They flow in deep cut gorges, sides of which are clothed with thick forests.

The eastern slopes of the Manipur eastern hills are washed by a number of small streams of the Chindwin system, which have a catchment of 6953 km^2, about 31.1 per cent area of the state. River Akonglok and its tributaries-Chamu and Chingai, and river

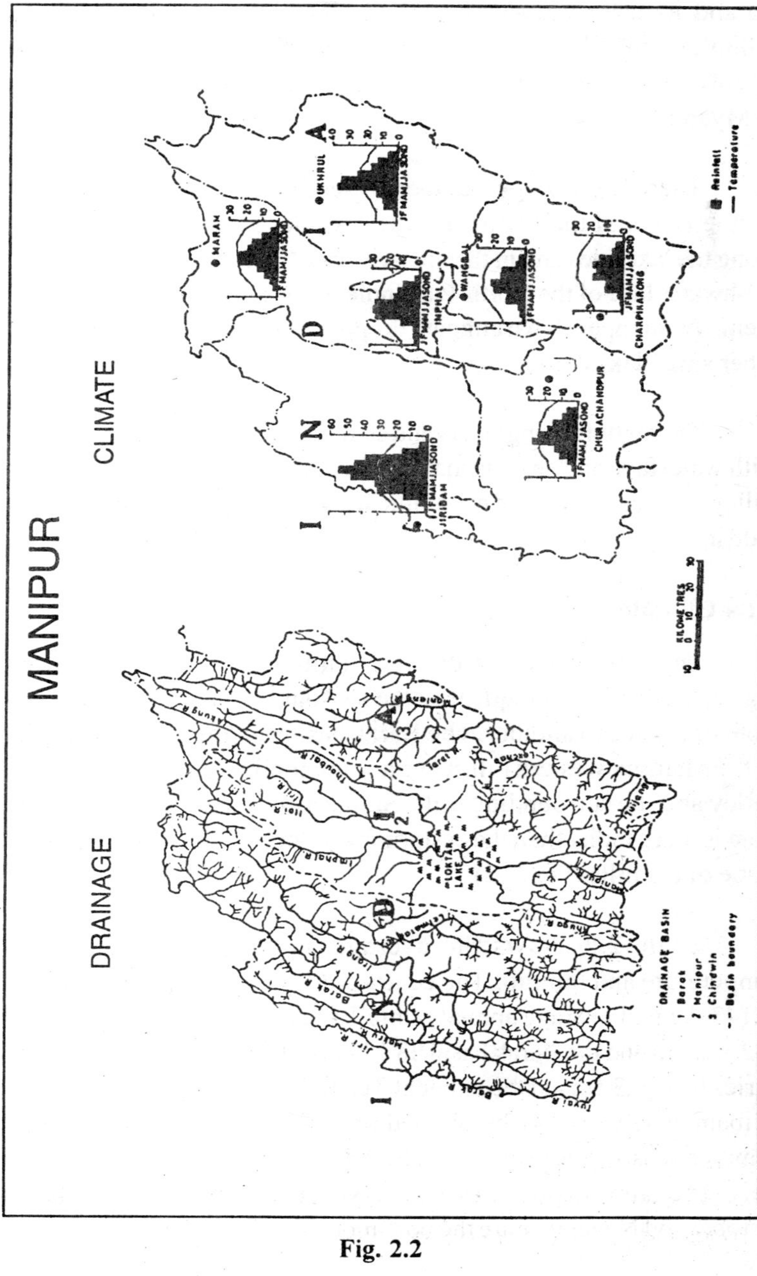
MANIPUR
DRAINAGE
CLIMATE
LOKTAK LAKE
DRAINAGE BASIN
1 Barak
2 Manipur
3 Chindwin
-- Basin boundary
KILOMETRES
UKHRUL
MARAM
IMPHAL
WANGBAL
JIRIBAM
CHURACHANDPUR
CHAKPIKARONG
Rainfall
Temperature

Fig. 2.2

Yu and its tributaries-Maklong, Tuyangbi, Taret Lok, Lokchao, Lalimlok and Tuiyang, flowing in sub-parallel pattern through their steeply cut valleys, join finally the Chindwin river in Kabaw valley in Myanmar.

There are a large number of large and small lakes in the southern part of the Manipur valley besides swamps and marshes along the lakesides and in the inter-riverine tracts. Loktak, the largest freshwater lake of the North-East India, is the most important among them. Pumlenpat, Kharungpat, Ikoppat and Waithoupat, etc. are other small lakes of the region (Fig. 2.2).

The swift flowing rivers and streams of the state are associated with waterfalls and springs in the hills, and lakes and marshes in the valley, and, as such, have economic importance for agricultural and industrial growth of Manipur.

2.1.4 Climate

The impact of terrain diversity, altitudinal variation and river regime has become eloquent in the seasonal variability of climate from one place to another. The Barak basin and the lower foothills of the Manipur western hills have a warmer climate than the central valley and the surrounding hills. Similarly, the western part of the state is more moist than the eastern for its location on the windward slope of the hills (Fig. 2.2).

Table 2.2 shows the average monthly distribution of temperature and rainfall. The central valley experiences 108.5 cm to 143.4 cm of average annual rainfall, the hill areas from 125.9 cm to 246.1 cm and the Barak basin 287.1 cm, while the monthly rainfall varies from 0.3 cm in December at Tengnoupal to 54.9 cm in July at Jiribam. The year may be divided broadly into four seasons. The summer season begins by March and extends upto the middle of May. The rainy season is from mid-May to the end of September. October and November are the post-monsoon or retreating monsoon

Table 2.2

Average Monthly Distribution of Temperature (^0C) and Rainfall (cm)

Station		Jan	Feb	Mar	Apr	May	Jun	Jul	Aug	Sep	Oct	Nov	Dec	Annual	Range of temperature
Imphal	T	12.4	14.7	18.8	22.1	24.0	25.0	25.1	25.1	24.8	22.5	17.6	13.5	20.4	12.7
	R	1.8	2.8	3.2	11.3	26.8	28.3	27.1	15.8	13.1	9.8	3.0	0.4	143.4	
Wangbal	T	12.9	15.1	18.5	22.2	24.7	25.7	25.6	25.8	25.5	22.4	18.2	13.7	20.9	12.9
	R	0.6	2.6	4.2	10.7	10.1	19.8	20.7	15.2	14.5	6.0	4.0	0.6	108.5	
Chura-	T	11.8	15.8	16.9	21.3	22.5	21.3	23.9	23.4	22.9	20.9	18.4	14.8	119.5	12.1
chandpur	R	0.4	2.0	5.0	9.8	12.7	27.2	22.9	18.3	14.4	9.2	6.7	0.4	129.0	
Thanlon	T	17.2	17.6	19.9	21.3	20.3	23.7	20.9	24.0	23.5	22.4	20.0	17.4	20.7	6.8
	R	1.2	3.2	7.7	20.9	28.9	45.1	43.5	37.6	34.9	15.7	6.5	0.9	246.1	
Chak-	T	18.2	20.0	22.4	25.5	26.1	28.2	28.1	28.3	28.4	26.3	22.9	19.3	24.5	10.2
pikarong	R	0.5	1.7	3.2	10.8	10.4	19.4	16.7	18.5	15.1	7.4	5.4	0.6	109.7	
Tengnou-	T	11.9	13.1	17.1	17.9	20.3	20.9	20.2	20.6	20.4	18.5	15.7	12.0	17.4	9.0
pal	R	0.9	2.5	2.5	10.9	18.2	36.8	53.3	38.6	31.4	16.6	9.5	0.3	221.5	
Ukhrul	T	13.2	13.2	14.9	17.3	19.8	21.5	21.8	22.0	22.7	18.9	17.9	14.6	18.2	9.5
	R	0.5	2.2	7.7	8.8	12.7	36.6	33.9	24.0	16.4	12.3	6.3	1.3	162.7	
Maram	T	13.5	15.5	18.7	21.8	22.9	24.5	24.6	24.8	25.0	22.9	20.3	14.1	20.7	11.5
	R	0.5	2.5	4.5	7.9	12.5	23.3	23.4	18.8	16.1	10.0	5.0	1.4	125.9	
Jiribam	T	16.3	18.1	22.0	24.9	27.8	28.9	30.4	29.9	28.5	25.0	21.9	17.8	24.3	14.1
	R	0.8	4.4	13.9	30.1	32.1	47.3	54.9	45.1	35.7	15.8	5.5	1.5	287.1	

Source : Meteorological Data of Manipur 1972-96

months and the period from December to the end of February is the winter season. The winter and summer seasons are generally dry, while the rainy and retreating monsoon seasons are moist.

The summer season starts with sudden increase of temperature, vanishing fog and occasional thunder showers. The early part of this season is the pleasant 'spring' season, the period of major festivals and dances in the state. The rainy season is associated with heavy rainfall, widespread cloudiness, high humidity and variable surface winds. The rains herald the beginning of the agricultural activities. The retreating monsoon season is marked by the gradual decline in rains, clear sky, short duration morning fogs and fair and pleasant weather besides bright sunny days and cool pleasant nights. The winter season, on the other hand, is characterised by cold nights, warm and windy days and foggy weather. The western depressions traverse the region during this period bringing a little rain of about 3-4 cm.

Although the state receives adequate rainfall for agricultural purposes, it suffers from its temporal variations. Intensive concentration of rainfall to a few rainy days causes flood, while too early or too late onset of the monsoon and long breaks delay the agricultural operations or damage the standing crops. This uncertainity is a major factor affecting the agricultural productivity.

2.1.5 Soils

The soils of the state (Fig. 2.3) belong to two major types-residual and transported, which cover the hill areas and the central valley respectively. The residual soils are either laterized or non-laterized. The laterized red soils (*Oxisol*), covering an area of 2500 km^2 in the Barak drainage on the western slopes of the Manipur western hills, are the original laterites formed at higher levels under the conditions of high rainfall with strongly expressed dry seasons. They contain a rich proportion of nitrogen and phosphate, a medium acidity and lesser amount of potash but respond well to manuring. The old alluviums of the Barak basin are the redeposited laterites

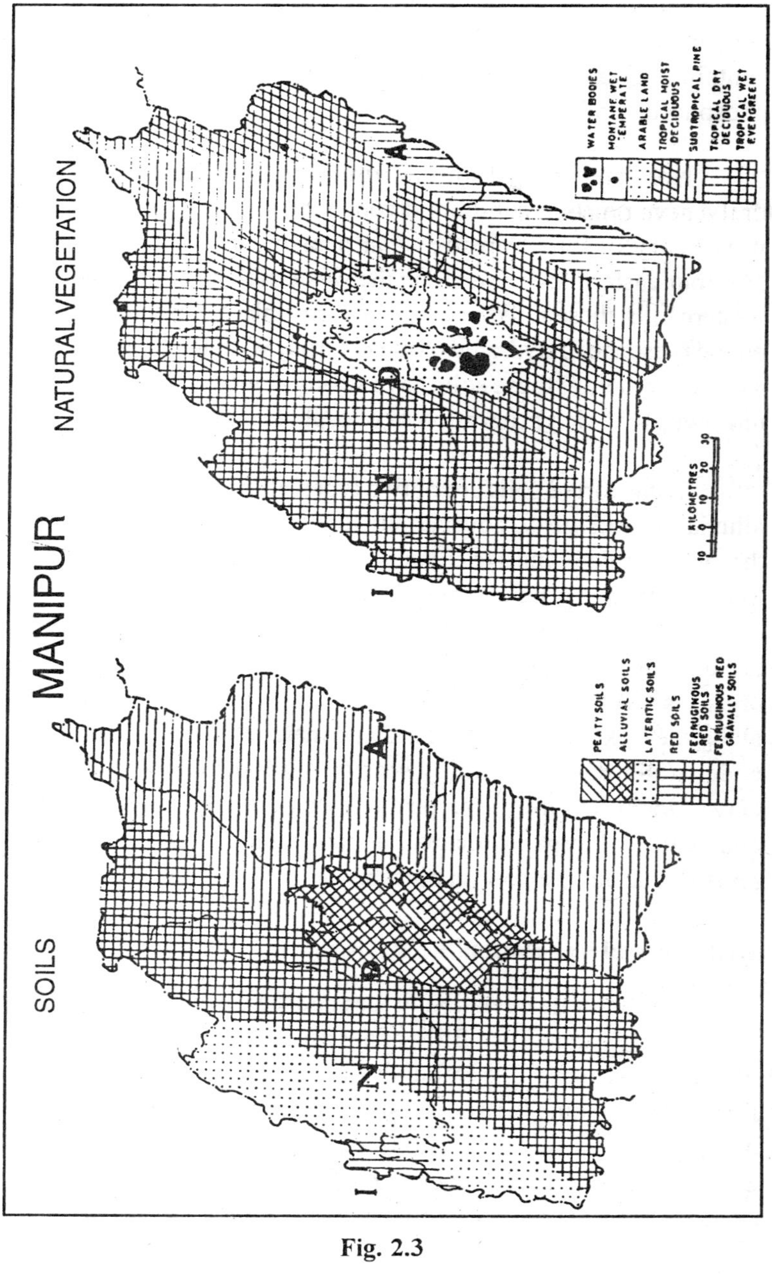
MANIPUR
SOILS
PEATY SOILS
ALLUVIAL SOILS
LATERITIC SOILS
RED SOILS
FERRUGINOUS RED SOILS
FERRUGINOUS RED GRAVALLY SOILS
NATURAL VEGETATION
WATER BODIES
MONTANE WET TEMPERATE
ARABLE LAND
TROPICAL MOIST DECIDUOUS
SUBTROPICAL PINE
TROPICAL DRY DECIDUOUS
TROPICAL WET EVERGREEN
KILOMETRES
10 0 10 20 30
INDIA
INDIA

Fig. 2.3

brought down by rivers Barak and Jiri and their tributaries from the neighbouring lateritic hills. These compact and less permeable soils contain higher quantity of potash, fair amount of nitrogen and phosphorus, and medium acidity.

Non-laterised red soils (*Ultisol*) are found in major parts of the Manipur hills, a sub-humid zone with alternating pronounced wet and dry seasons. Spread over an area of 17800 km^2 in the entire Manipur eastern hills and along the western flanks of the Manipur western hills, these soils vary in colour from place to place depending on the presence of hydrated oxides of iron. With loamy texture and granular structure these soils have strong acidity, a fair quantity of nitrogen and a rich proportion of phosphate and potash.

Transported soils are of two types-alluvial and organic. The alluvial soils (*Entisol*) cover about 1600 km^2 in the Manipur valley, the most populous and agriculturally well-developed part of the state. These soils have general clayey loam texture and grey to pale brown colour. They contain a good proportion of potash and phosphate, a fair quantity of nitrogen and organic matter and are less acidic. The organic soils (*Histosol*) cover the low-lying areas of the central valley along the Loktak and other lakes and marshes. These soils remain under water during the rainy season. With dark grey colour and clayey loam texture, these peaty or bog soils have high acidity, abundance of organic matter, a good amount of nitrogen and phosphorus but are poor in potash.

2.1.6 Natural Vegetation

The natural vegetation in the state mainly consists of forests which occupy about four-fifths of her geographical area. The forests of Manipur are spread over four distinct zones, viz. Myanmar border forests, Ukhrul pine forests, forests overlooking the valley and Barak drainage forests, and belong to five different types (Champion and Seth, 1968)- (i) tropical wet evergreen, (ii) tropical moist deciduous, (iii) sub-tropical pine, (iv) tropical dry deciduous, and (v) montane wet temperate forests (Fig. 2.3).

Tropical wet evergreen forests are usually found in the north-western, western and south-western parts of Manipur which produce canes and bamboos abundantly in the Barak drainage area-in Tamenglong and Churachandpur districts. Besides 13 major species of bamboos, these forests contain timber species like *Haldi, Siris, Chaplash, Aini, Agar, Toon, Jarul, Bonsum* and mango.

Table 2.3
Manipur : Classification of Forests, 1999

Classification by	Area (Km^2)	Percentage to total Geographical area	Percentage to total Forest area
A. Legal status :			
Reserved forests	1467	6.57	8.33
Protected forests	4171	18.68	23.67
Unclassed forests	11983	53.67	68.00
B. Composition :			
Coniferous forests	2442	10.94	13.86
Broad-leaved forests	9444	42.30	53.59
Pure bamboo brakes	3268	14.63	18.55
Bamboo Clumps	2467	11.05	14.00
C. Function :			
Production forests	3415	15.30	19.38
Under exploitation forests	4118	18.44	23.37
Potentially exploitable forests	10088	45.18	57.25
D. Group :			
Tree forests	11740	52.58	66.62
Bamboo forests	3268	14.63	18.55
Grass blank/barren	2613	11.71	14.83

E. Vegetation :			
Wet temperate forests	1451	6.50	8.23
Pine forests	2443	10.94	13.86
Wet hill forests	9057	40.57	51.40
Semi-evergreen forests	645	2.89	3.66
Teak *Gurjan* forests	611	2.74	3.47
Bamboo brakes	3268	14.63	18.55
Grassy blanks	146	0.65	0.83
Total	17621	78.92	100.00

Source : Forest Department, Government of Manipur.

Tropical moist deciduous forests are found in and around the central valley and extend upto Indo-Myanmar border to the east. Important timber species found in these forests include oak, teak, *Kangin, Khen* and *Toon*. Teak trees in this part do not attain large size because of poor forest management. Giant creepers girdle the trees and ruin the stems.

Sub-tropical pine forests are found in the northeastern part of Ukhrul, south-eastern part of Tamenglong and some portion of Chandel and Churachandpur districts. The altitudinal zone of these forests is between 1200 to 1500 m above the mean sea level. Pine trees, particularly the Khasia Pine, with important species of orchids including Siroi Lily are found in the area alongwith oak and chestnut trees.

Tropical dry deciduous forests found along the Myanmar border are continuation of the teak forests of Kabaw valley. Teak, *Kangin* and *Khen* are important timber species found in these forests. Montane wet temperate forests are found in pockets at Siroi, Mao and Koubru at a height of about 1800-2400 m and contain evergreen species with predominance of oak and pine trees, which widely vary in size due to altitudinal differences.

Table 2.3 shows the classification of forests in Manipur according to their legal status, composition, function, group and vegetation.

Though forests cover 78.92 per cent area of Manipur, they contribute less than two per cent to the net domestic product of the state. Timber, particularly teak, bamboo and cane grow abundantly in the forests in the state. With decreasing production, represented by revenue receipts, and everincreasing expenditure on their maintenance (Table 2.4), the forests, which would have provided a face-lift to the state economy, have become a burden on the state exchequer.

Table 2.4
Revenue Receipts and Expenditure on Forests

(Rs. in lakhs)

Year	Receipt	Expenditure
1960-61	4.14	3.30
1970-71	4.10	13.89
1980-81	29.28	152.39
1990-91	101.01	1005.63
1995-96	223.48	1645.95
1998-99	70.47	1558.68

Source : Forest Department, Government of Manipur.

The forests are depleted mostly by the people living in the hills for shifting cultivation, firewood and timber every year which is bound to create ecological imbalances in the state.

2.2 Economic Structure

Manipur is endowed with natural resources-the lush-green

Table 2.5

Manipur : Major Land Use Categories, 1988-89

(in percentage)

Category	District								Manipur
	Imphal East/West	Thoubal	Bishnupur	Senapati	Tamenglong	Churachandpur	Chandel	Ukhrul	
Built-up land	3.96	0.65	0.81	0.10	0.06	0.16	0.11	0.14	0.35
Built-up land with plantations	10.40	14.27	3.72	-	-	0.37	-	-	1.05
Cropland of *Kharif* season	64.48	42.75	56.93	5.11	0.80	2.54	1.27	0.76	7.58
Agricultural plantations	0.34	-	-	-	-	-	-	-	0.02
Shifting cultivation	14.06	10.08	3.26	42.43	15.37	26.96	19.77	15.80	21.97
Evergreen/semi-evergreen forest	-	-	-	1.30	8.32	0.92	-	3.01	2.63
Deciduous forest	-	-	-	-	-	0.70	1.91	0.83	0.59
Degraded forest or scrub land	-	6.93	-	51.06	75.45	68.35	76.94	79.46	64.05
Marshy/Swampy land	6.25	23.72	17.87	-	-	-	-	-	1.29
Water bodies	0.51	1.60	17.41	-	-	-	-	-	0.47
Area (in km^2)	1228	514	496	3271	4391	4570	3313	4544	22327

Source : Report on land Use/Land Cover Manipur State 1988-89.

forests in the hills, fertile alluvial soils in the river basins, swift-flowing rivers and streams, a large number of fresh water lakes including the Loktak, and an optimum climate affecting the economic growth of the state. The fertile river valleys of Manipur are well-suited for agriculture and horticulture, the waterbodies and marshes for fisheries and poultry, the foothills for livestock and dairying and the hill areas with rich forests and minerals for the development of industries.

2.2.1 Land Use

The major land use/land cover categories identified in the state are built-up land, built-up land with plantations, cropland of *Kharif* season, agricultural plantation, evergreen/semi-evergreen and deciduous forests, degraded forest or scrub land, marshy/swampy land, water-bodies and shifting cultivation areas (NRSA, 1990). Table 2.5 shows their percentage distribution districtwise in the state, while Fig. 2.4 portrays their spatial distribution.

Agriculture varies in different parts of the state with differences in terrain, climate and edaphic factors. The cropped areas are mostly found in the central valley, Barak basin, valley floor in the hills, hill slopes and on the piedmont areas. Agricultural plantation like tea is found on the piedomont slopes in the south-western part of Jiribam subdivision. Shifting cultivation is extensively practised in the hill districts. Degraded jhumlands in the western hills contain bamboos and canes. Evergreen and semi-evergreen forests cover the western part of the state and small patches in the northern part of Senapati district and eastern part of Ukhrul district. The deciduous forests occur in the eastern part of Chandel, Ukhrul and Churachandpur districts.

Marshy/swampy land is the major wasteland category in the valley districts around the Loktak lake. Settlements in the state are often found mixed with plantations. These occur as linear patches on the river banks, on the margins of the lakes and by roadside in

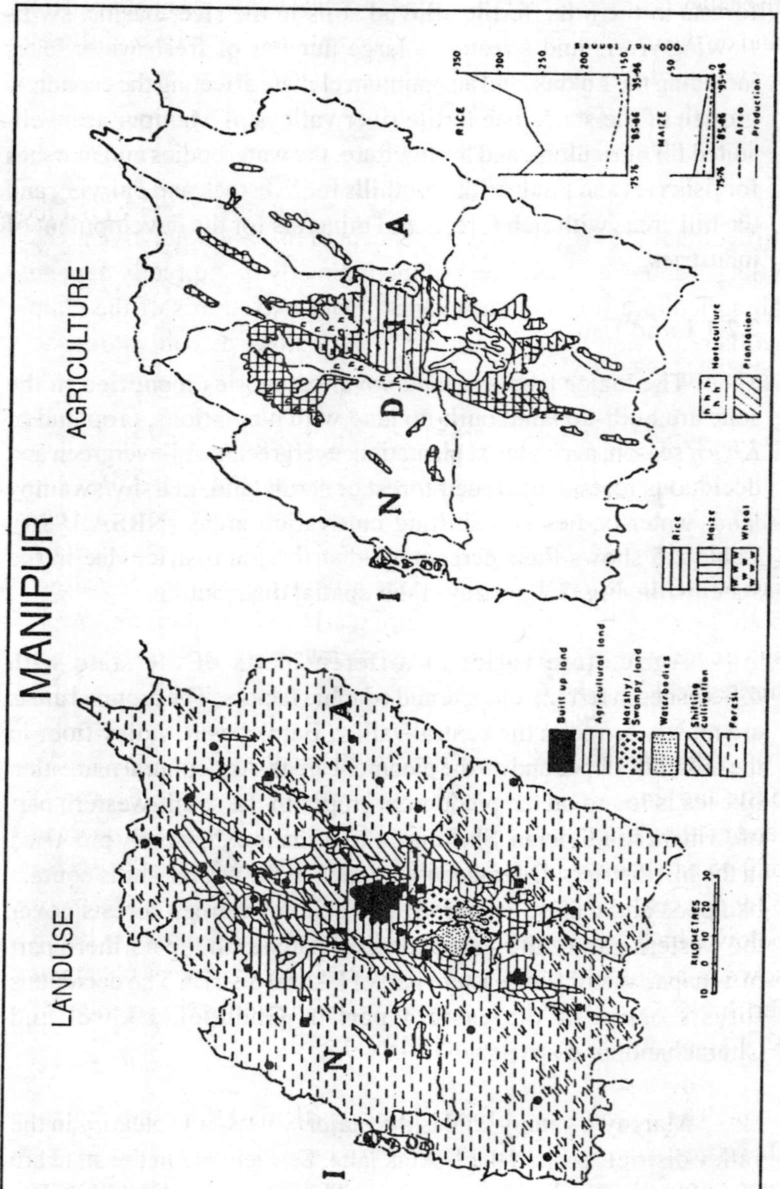
MANIPUR
LANDUSE
AGRICULTURE
Built up land
Agricultural land
Marshy/ Swampy land
Waterbodies
Shifting cultivation
Forest
KILOMETRES
10 0 10 20 30
Rice
Maize
Wheat
Horticulture
Plantation
RICE
MAIZE
Area
Production
INDIA

Fig. 2.4

the valley. The settlements along the riverside follow a sinuous pattern and on the roadside a straight line. The settlements on the hill slopes and ridges have scattered locations.

2.2.2 Agriculture

Agriculture occupies the most important place in the economic structure of the state. About 72 per cent of its population live in the villages and over 70 per cent of them directly or indirectly depend on agriculture for their sustenance. Over two- thirds of the main workers in Manipur are engaged in agriculture as cultivators and agricultural labourers.

The cropping pattern in the state is typical of an underdeveloped agricultural economy with about four-fifths of the total cultivated area under cereals, mainly rice. Double cropping of rice is practised in the central valley with the help of irrigation facilities. Maize, grown mainly in the hills on the jhumlands, pulses-both *Rabi* and *Kharif*, oilseeds-particularly mustard and sunflower, sugarcane and wheat are grown in various parts of the state on a limited scale.

Settled farming is practised in the central valley and Barak basin and shifting cultivation (*Jhuming*) in the hill tracts. Per capita land holding in the state is barely 0.10 ha against the national average of 0.15 ha. About 83.8 per cent of the land holdings, accounting for 62.9 per cent of the total cultivated land, falls in the category of below 2 ha holding size. High yielding variety of seeds are being sown in about half of the cultivated land and the use of chemical fertilizers per hectare is 49.8 kg as against the all-India average of 67.1 kg (North Eastern Council, 1995).

The production of food-grains, particularly rice and maize, fluctuates sharply from year to year (Fig. 2.4) according to the success or failure of the crops, which depend mainly on the capricious rainfall. Flash floods followed by dry spells of drought and vice versa have become an almost regular feature in the state affecting the agricultural productivity. As such, irrigation facilities play an important role in agricultural operations, but assured irrigation facilities are available for only about two-fifths of the cultivated land. Imphal West district has got the highest irrigated area and Chandel district the least.

Table 2.6

Area and Production of Rice and Maize in Manipur

Year	Rice		Maize	
	Area ('000 ha)	Production ('000 tonnes)	Area ('000 ha)	Production ('000 tonnes)
1980-81	171.85	249.19	9.91	17.78
1985-86	164.60	268.08	5.74	14.63
1990-91	157.41	274.17	4.61	11.40
1995-96	134.93	338.05	2.55	7.05
1998-99	166.89	382.19	2.96	10.09

Source : Directorate of Economics and Statistics, Govt. of Manipur.

2.2.3 Horticulture

The state is well suited for development of horticulture due to its varied relief and climate. However, only 5.14 per cent of the total cultivated land is used for fruit crops and 6.13 per cent for vegetables and spices. The central valley is ideally suitable for fruits like papaya, banana and mango, and the hill areas for pineapple, orange, banana, pear, peach and lemon.

Orange, banana, lemon and cashewnut grow well on the western hills, specially in Tamenglong district. Pear, peach and plum are grown in Senapati and Ukhrul districts. Pineapple, a moisture conserving and erosion resisting plant, is widely grown on the hill slopes in Senapati, Churachandpur and Chandel districts and on the hillsides bordering the valley.

Table 2.7
Livestock and Poultry in Manipur, 1997

District	Livestock								Poultry
	Cattle	Buffaloe	*Mithun*	Sheep/ Goat	Horses/ Ponies	Pigs	Dogs/ others	Total	
Imphal East/West	159442	5470	-	4895	1040	20257	28467	219571	925508
	(31.37)	(5.74)		(12.09)	(44.69)	(5.22)	(19.24)	(18.31)	(30.28)
Thoubal	80755	7384	-	2820	302	22078	20620	133359	321556
	(15.89)	(7.75)		(6.97)	(12.98)	(5.69)	(13.94)	(11.17)	(10.52)
Bishnupur	53222	3797	-	426	215	5907	6500	70067	323478
	(10.47)	(3.99)		(1.05)	(9.24)	(1.52)	(4.39)	(5.84)	(10.58)
Senapati	103384	38226	853	21430	125	141352	41731	347101	468229
	(20.34)	(40.13)	(5.12)	(52.95)	(5.37)	(36.43)	(28.20)	(28.95)	(15.32)
Tamenglong	27745	8224	1908	7132	43	53561	17321	115934	241808
	(5.46)	(8.64)	(11.45)	(17.62)	(1.85)	(13.80)	(11.71)	(9.67)	(7.91)
Churachandpur	18374	5223	1283	1784	314	31560	5110	63648	215427
	(3.62)	(5.48)	(7.70)	(4.41)	(13.49)	(8.13)	(3.45)	(5.31)	(7.04)
Chandel	35487	6308	2938	881	239	69518	17897	133268	275292
	(6.98)	(6.62)	(17.64)	(2.18)	(10.27)	(17.91)	(12.10)	(11.12)	(9.01)
Ukhrul	29855	20617	9678	1107	49	43838	10319	115458	285336
	(5.87)	(21.65)	(58.09)	(2.73)	(2.11)	(11.30)	(6.97)	(9.63)	(9.34)
Manipur	508264	95249	16660	40475	2327	388066	147965	1199006	3056634
	(100.00)	(100.00)	(100.00)	(100.00)	(100.00)	(100.00)	(100.00)	(100.00)	(100.00)

Source : Sixteenth Quinquennial Census of Livestock, 1997.

A large variety of vegetables and spices like potato, peas, cabbage, cauliflower, brinjal, tomato, pumpkin, chillies and ginger cover a considerable part of the valley as well as the hills, but grown mostly for domestic needs in the kitchen gardens attached to the settled areas. Chillies and ginger are cultivated on commercial scale in Churachandpur district and potato in Tamenglong district.

2.2.4 Livestock and Fisheries

The livestock and fisheries in the state, though quite large in number cannot be considered satisfactory as regards the quality. The animal wealth of Manipur consists of cattle, buffaloes, sheep, goats, horses, pigs and other domestic animals besides poultry and fish. Among them, the cattle, buffaloes and pigs are the most important. Cattle and buffaloes provide motive power in the wet cultivation. Pigs and poultry are reared by the hill people and the scheduled caste section of society in the valley. Table 2.7 shows the number of livestock and poultry in Manipur.

Cattle are found in large number in Imphal East, Imphal West, Senapati and Thoubal districts; buffaloes in Senapati and Ukhrul districts; *Mithun* in Ukhrul and Chandel districts; sheep and goat in Senapati and Tamenglong districts; horses and ponies in Imphal East, Imphal West, Churachandpur and Thoubal districts, pigs in Senapati, Chandel and Tamenglong districts and dogs in Senapati and Imphal East and Imphal West districts. Poultry birds are reared throughout the state but with larger concentration in Imphal East, Imphal West and Senapati districts (Fig. 2.5). The indigenous cows and buffaloes are of poor breed affecting the milk production, which is around 64.74 tonnes per annum at present.

The state abounds in lakes and marshes, rivers and streams, which form considerable fishing grounds. Fishing is an important occupation of the rural population living around the Loktak and other lakes in the valley. But fish production (Table 2.8) from these fisheries is far short of the requirements.

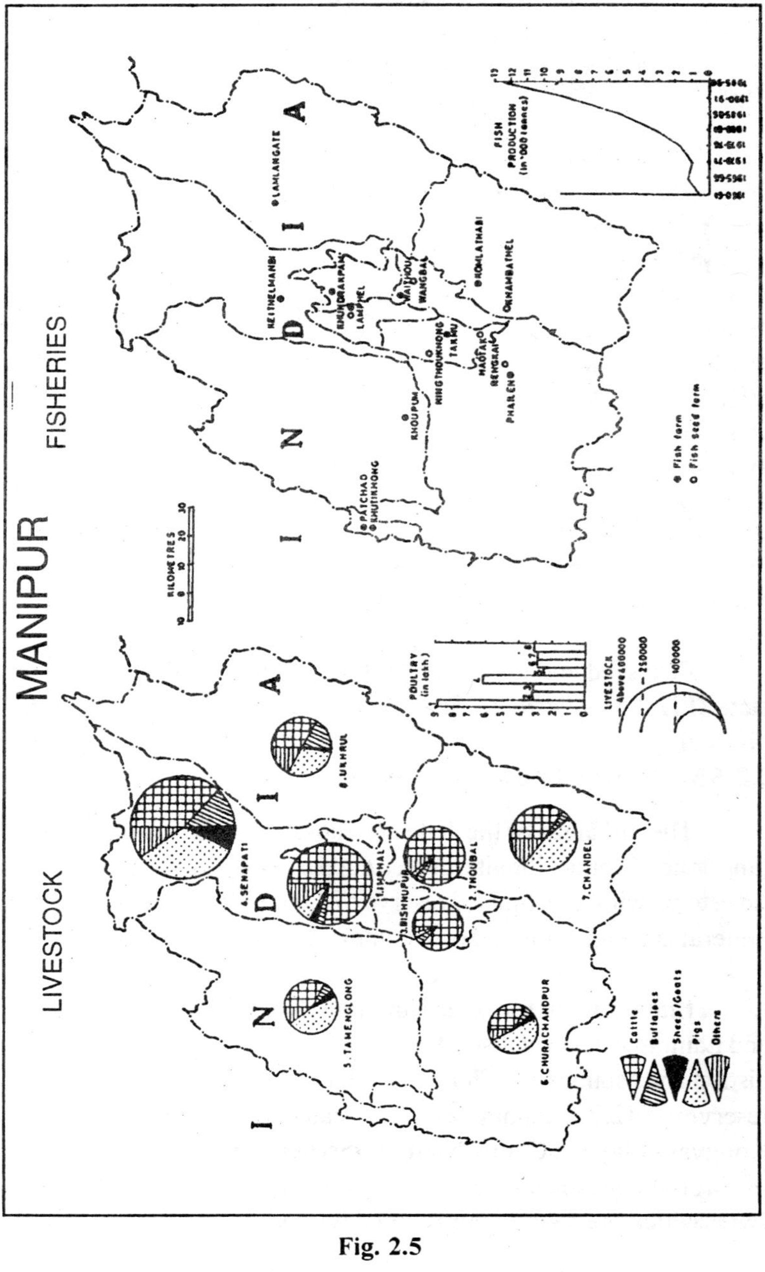
MANIPUR
LIVESTOCK
FISHERIES
INDIA
KILOMETRES
POULTRY (in lakh)
LIVESTOCK
FISH PRODUCTION (in '000 tonnes)
Cattle
Buffaloes
Sheep/Goats
Pigs
Others
Fish farm
Fish seed farm
4. SENAPATI
8. UKHRUL
5. TAMENGLONG
6. CHURACHANDPUR
7. CHANDEL
2. THOUBAL
3. BISHNUPUR
1. IMPHAL
LAMLANGATE
KEITHELMANBI
LAMPHEL
WAITHOU
WANGBAL
IKOP
KHOUPUM
PHAILENG
IHUTIKHONG

Fig. 2.5

Table.2.8

Production of Fish in Manipur

Year	Fish seed farm	Experimental fish farm	Fish production (in tonnes)	Estimated fish requirement (in tonnes)
1960-61	4	-	511	4100
1965-66	4	-	1260	4800
1970-71	4	-	1000	7700
1975-76	8	-	1800	9000
1980-81	9	-	3250	7600
1985-86	14	3	5500	8600
1990-91	14	3	8500	18000
1995-96	14	3	12502	20513
1998-99	14	3	15,309	20,000

Source : Directorate of Fisheries, Government of Manipur.

Fish seed and experimental farms, scattered throughout the state (Fig.2.5), distribute fingerlings and provide impetus to the pisciculturists.

2.2.5 Mineral and Power Resources

The hill areas of the state are endowed with rich deposits of limestone, chromite, lignite, nickel, copper, asbestos and salt. Except limestone, with an estimated reserve of 8.09 million tonnes, no other mineral is being exploited on a commercial scale.

Limestone is found at Hundung, Khankhui, Mova, Kasom and Lambui in Ukhrul district, Pallel-Chakpikarong belt of Chandel district and Monbung in Churachandpur district. Lignite with proved reserves of 12,200 tonnes has been located in the stream basin near Kongvai village in Churachandpur district. Considerable quantity of chromite, nickel, copper and asbestos have been estimated in the state, which are found mainly in Ukhrul and Chandel districts. A

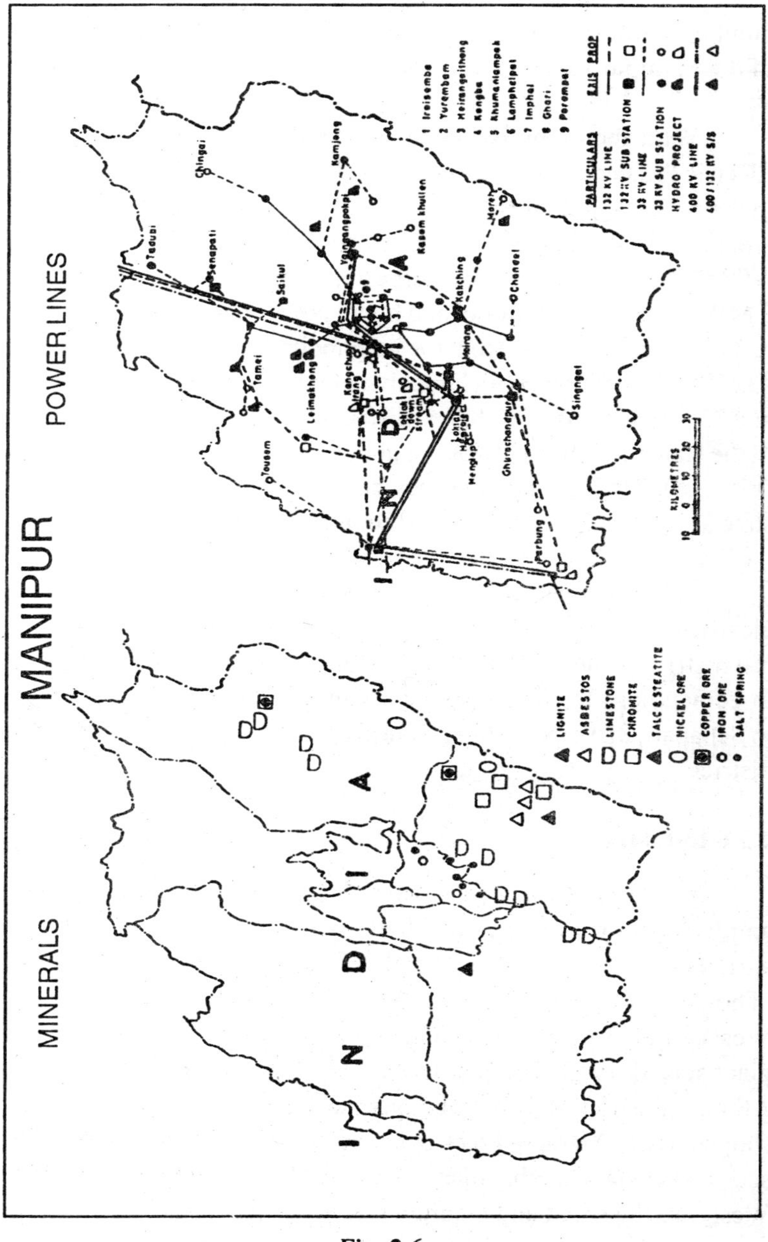
MANIPUR
MINERALS
POWER LINES
LIGNITE
ASBESTOS
LIMESTONE
CHROMITE
TALC & STEATITE
NICKEL ORE
COPPER ORE
IRON ORE
SALT SPRING
1 Iroisemba
2 Yurembam
3 Meirangeithong
4 Kongba
5 Khumanlampak
6 Lamphelpat
7 Imphal
8 Ghari
9 Parompat
PARTICULARS
EXIS
PROP
132 KV LINE
132 KV SUB STATION
33 KV LINE
33 KV SUB STATION
HYDRO PROJECT
400 KV LINE
400/132 KV S/S
KILOMETRES

Fig. 2.6

number of salt springs occur along the foot-hills in the eastern part of the Manipur valley (Fig. 2.6).

With the commissioning of the 105 MW Loktak Hydro-Electric Project in 1984, the state has shown a marked improvement in the power supply position. The peak load demand of the state is around 117 MW, of which it receives 50 MW from the Loktak Power Grid System, and to meet its increasing demands it generates about 3 MW of power from diesel and hydel power plants and purchases rest of its requirements from the neighbouring states. There are six 132 KV sub-stations which receive power from the Grid System, and 33 sub-stations of 33 KV to distribute power to different places in the state through a network of about 2373 of 11 KV sub-stations (Fig. 2.6). The per capita energy consumption is 165 units in the state as against 330 units for the country as a whole.

While all the settlements in the Manipur valley have been electrified, only 192 of them have not been electrified so far in the hill districts, where rural electrification varies from 56.19 per cent in Tamenglong to 68.73 per cent in Churachandpur, 78.96 per cent in Senapati, 81.98 per cent in Ukhrul and 84.93 per cent in Chandel district.

2.2.6 Industry

Industrially the state is least developed even though it has ample scope to develop industries based on forest, mineral and agricultural resources. The Khandsari Sugar Factory at Khangabok (Thoubal), Manipur Spinning Mill at Loitang Khunou (Imphal West), Mini Cement Plant at Hundung (Ukhrul), bamboo chipping plant at Kadamtala, Jiribam (Imphal East), Manipur Vanaspati and Allied Industries and drug and pharmaceuticals plant at Nilakuthi (Imphal East), Manipur Electronics, assembling television and radio sets, and cycle assembly plants at Takyel Industrial Estate (Imphal West) are the small and medium size industries established in the state (Fig. 2.7) as part of the programme for the diversification of

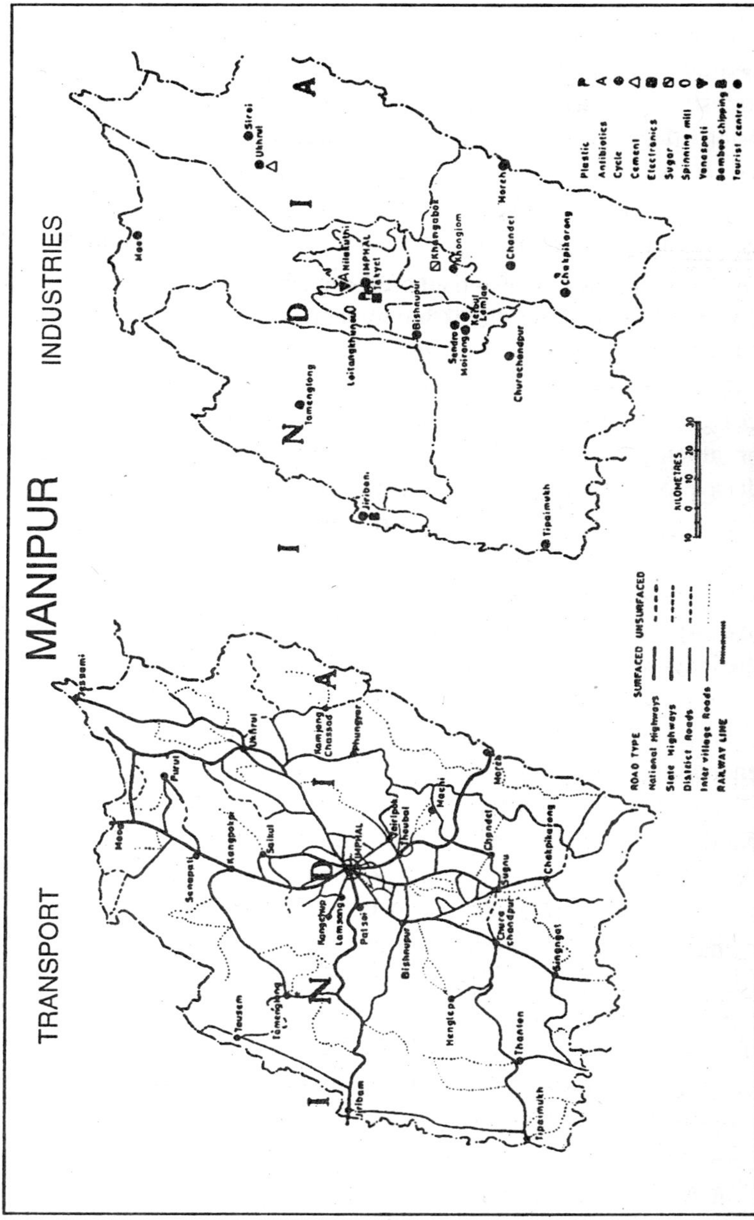
MANIPUR
TRANSPORT
INDUSTRIES
ROAD TYPE
SURFACED
UNSURFACED
National Highways
State Highways
District Roads
Inter village Roads
RAILWAY LINE
KILOMETRES
Plastic
Antibiotics
Cycle
Cement
Electronics
Sugar
Spinning mill
Vanaspati
Bamboo chipping
Tourist centre

Fig. 2.7

economy and creation of additional employment opportunities. Besides these industries, there are a large number of agro-based industries such as rice mills, saw mills, flour and *dal* mills alongwith brick kilns in different parts of the valley and the hills.

Among the non-agricultural activities, household industry is the most important. Handloom weaving in the central valley and loinloom weaving in the hill areas are the oldest and universal cottage industries, which have become an integral part of the traditional culture of the people. The Manipuri women on their looms weave wide range of colourful clothes and shawls of intricate geometrical designs. Embroidery, metalware, cane and bamboo works, doll and ornament manufacturing are among important handicrafts. Earlier these products were largely confined to the domestic needs, but now they are important items of export to the national and international markets. If organised on commercial line with proper infrastructural support, handloom and handicrafts sector may provide employment to a large number of people, particularly women, besides augmenting the income of those already employed in the profession.

With its scenic beauty of the sparkling lakes and forest-clad enchanting hills, wildlife, historic monuments, temples and world famous dances - both classical and folk, handloom fabrics and handicrafts offer a wide variety of attractions to the tourists visiting this beautiful tract of the country. Most of the scenic spots of the state are located along the Loktak lake which include Moirang (INA complex), Sendra (tourist complex), Keibul Lamjao National Park (famous for its brow-antlered deer - *Sangai*) and Bishnupur (Vishnu temple), besides the floating huts in the lake water, the home and hearth of the fishermen. Imphal has its own tourist attractions such as Shree Govindjee temple, the temporal seat of the Vaishnavite culture, historic Kangla fort, Pologround, Second World War cemetries, *Shaheed Minar*, world famous women's market, Canchipur etc. Khnogjom war memorial, Kaina, Siroi (famous for unique Siroi lily), Ukhrul, Mao, Tamenglong, Jiribam, Churachandpur, Tipaimukh, Chandel, Chakpikarong and Morch are

Table 2.9
Length of Roads in Manipur, 1997

(in km.)

District	National Highway	State Highway	Major District Roads	Other District Roads	Inter village Roads	Municipal Roads	Total	Roads per 100 km^2
Imphal East/West	53	150	118	180	759	132	1392	113
Thoubal	35	94	21	203	469	-	822	160
Bishnupur	-	39	51	96	261	-	447	90
Senapati	115	50	49	152	499	-	865	26
Tamenglong	167	160	285	167	557	-	1336	30
Churachandpur	-	392	187	17	319	-	915	20
Chandel	64	30	48	100	258	-	500	15
Ukhrul	-	447	174	98	909	-	1628	36
Manipur	434	1362	933	1013	4031	132	7905	35

Source : Public Works Department, Government of Manipur.

other places of tourist importance in the state exhibiting religious, cultural and economic strength of the state (Fig. 2.7).

2.2.7 Transport and Communication

The existing transport network of 7,905 km of road length and 1.35 km of railways cannot be regarded adequate for the state with diverse terrain and ecology. The road density of 35 km per 100 km^2, is less than two-thirds of the national average of 55 km. Only 40 per cent of the villages are connected by road while many block and subdivisional headquarters are still not connected with district headquarters or state capital by all-weather roads.

On all-India pattern, the roads have been classified into six categories-National Highway, State Highway, major district roads, other district roads, inter-village roads and municipal roads (Table 2.9). The National Highways 39 and 53 connects the state with the neighbouring states of Nagaland and Assam. The recently declared National Highway 150, with a stretch of 523 km, connects Imphal with Kohima via Ukhrul and Aizawl via Churachandpur and Tipaimukh. The state highways connect the district headquarters with Imphal and the district roads block and subdivisional headquarters with the district headquarters. The inter-village roads, mostly unsurfaced, connect the villages with each other and join the nearest district roads and state highways while the municipal roads connect various parts of Imphal city (Fig. 2.7).

The central valley has a well integrated road network but the hill districts are less accessible for sparse road-net with many missing links. About one-fourth of roads are unsurfaced and are used only during the fair weather. The roads in general are of poor quality and need improvement in their surface structure.

In Jiribam subdivision, rivers Jiri and Barak provide effective water transport system for movement of goods and people. Jiribam is linked with Silchar in Assam by a metre gauge railway. People living around the Loktak lake and in the island settlements and

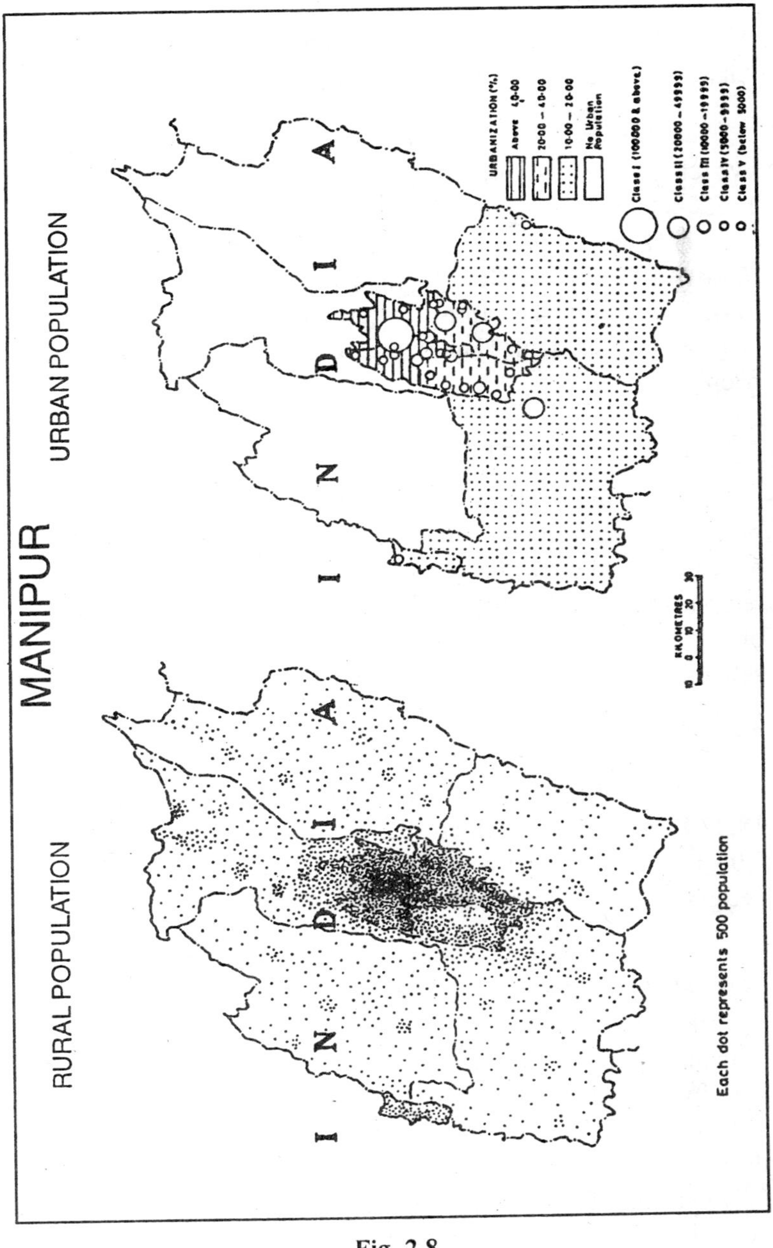
MANIPUR
RURAL POPULATION
URBAN POPULATION
I N D I A
I N D I A
Each dot represents 500 population
URBANIZATION (%)
KILOMETRES

Fig. 2.8

floating huts use canoes and small boats for inter-village transport. Airways link Imphal with Calcutta, Guwahati, Silchar and Delhi.

There are 676 post offices including one head post office, two telegraph offices, 48 combined post and telegraph offices, over 18650 telephones and over 1134 public call offices besides a large number of PCOs run by the individuals. Imphal has a medium wave radio station and a Doordarshan Kendra. A large number of newspapers published from Imphal and Churachandpur, both in English and vernacular languages, dessiminate information to the people.

2.3 Cultural Characteristics

Cultural profile of a region can be inferred from the spread of its population and lay-out of its settlements, which in turn affect each other and are affected by the geo-economic structure of the region. This section, as such, deals with the cultural characteristics of the state-its population, occupational composition, social traits, settlement pattern and social facilities.

2.3.1 Population

According to 1991 census, Manipur has a population of 18,37,149 persons, of which 13,31,504 live in the rural areas and 5,05, 645 in the urban tracts. Its density of population of 82 persons per km^2 is less than one-third of all-India density of 267 persons.

Four districts of the central valley-Imphal East, Imphal West, Thoubal and Bishnupur have large concentration of population, while the hill districts-Senapati, Churachandpur, Ukhrul, Chandel and Tamenglong have sparse and scattered spread of population (Fig. 2.8). In the Manipur valley, which covers only 9.26 per cent of the state area, live 62.70 per cent of population. In the Barak basin, on the western outskirts of the state, live 1.85 per cent of the people on 0.77 per cent of the state area, while in the Manipur hills 35.45 per cent of the state population resides over 89.97 per cent of the state area (Table 2.10). The hill areas have poor economic growth and

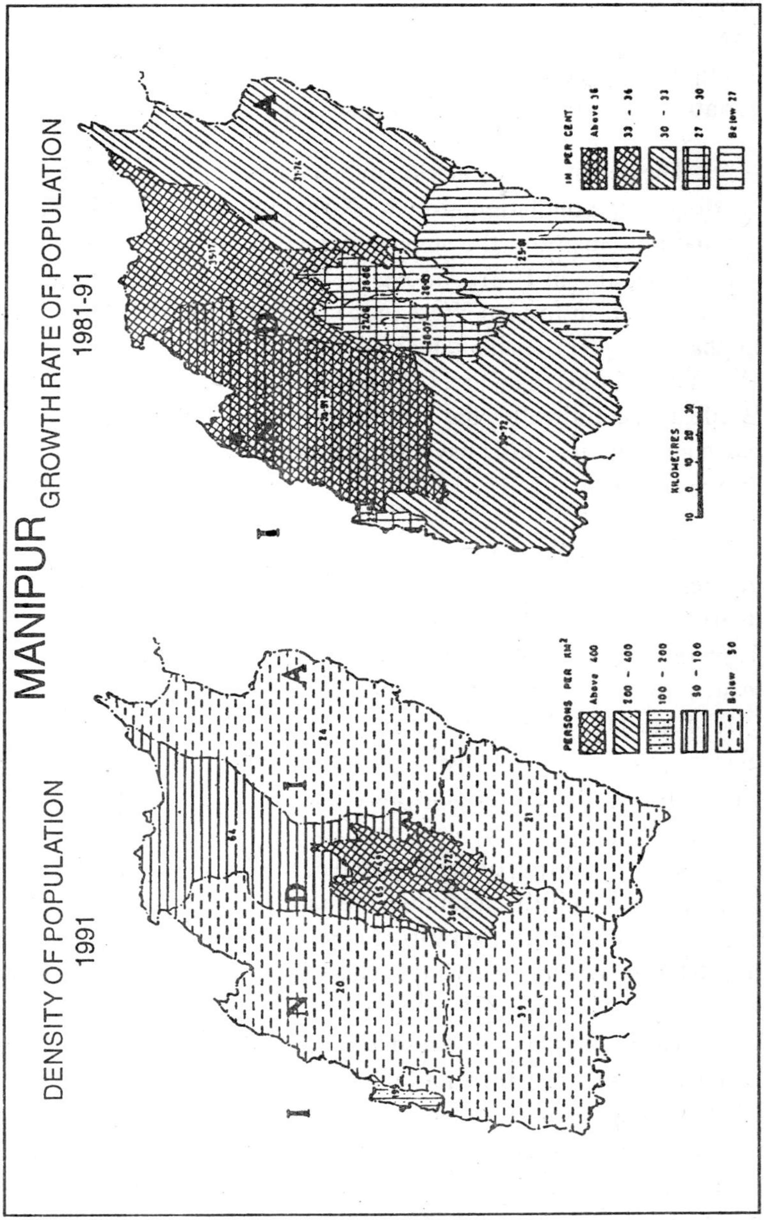
MANIPUR
DENSITY OF POPULATION
1991
GROWTH RATE OF POPULATION
1981-91
PERSONS PER KM²
Above 400
200 - 400
100 - 200
50 - 100
Below 50
IN PER CENT
Above 36
33 - 36
30 - 33
27 - 30
Below 27
KILOMETRES
INDIA
INDIA

Fig. 2.9

underutilisation of their vast natural resources and consequently a poor density of population. Thus, the distribution of population in Manipur is closely linked with the character of terrain, climatic variations and the pattern of land use (Fig. 2.8).

The density of population indicates the pressure on land and is affected by population growth. During the decade 1981-91, the population density in the state increased from 64 in 1981 to 82 persons per km^2 in 1991. Among the districts, the highest density was recorded in Imphal West (686) followed by Thoubal (572), Imphal East (491), Bishnupur (364), Senapati (64), Churachandpur (39), Ukhrul (24), Chandel (21) and Tamenglong (20) (Fig. 2.9). While the central valley has a population density of 555, the Barak basin and Manipur hills have densities of 199 and 32 persons per km^2 respectively.

The decadal growth rate in the state during 1981-91 was 29.29 per cent as against 23.85 per cent for the entire country. The hill districts recorded much higher growth than the valley districts. Tamenglong, with 38.51 per cent growth, registered the highest growth in the state followed by Senapati (34.09 per cent), Ukhrul (31.74 per cent) and Churachandpur (30.72 per cent). Chandel district experienced the lowest growth, only 25.81 per cent, and the valley districts below the state average (Fig. 2.9).

The proportion of urban population in the state in 1991 was 27.52 per cent, a little larger than the national average of 26.13 per cent. In the hill areas, the ratio of urban population is hardly one-fourth of the state average while in the valley it is 44 per cent higher.

Tamenglong, Ukhrul and Senapati districts in the northern hill tracts of the state have no urban settlements, and in Churachandpur and Chandel districts, with one town each, the proportion of urban population is too low, only 19.11 and 13.62 per cent respectively. The level of urbanisation ranges from 22.94 per cent in Imphal East to 56.69 per cent in Imphal West in the valley,

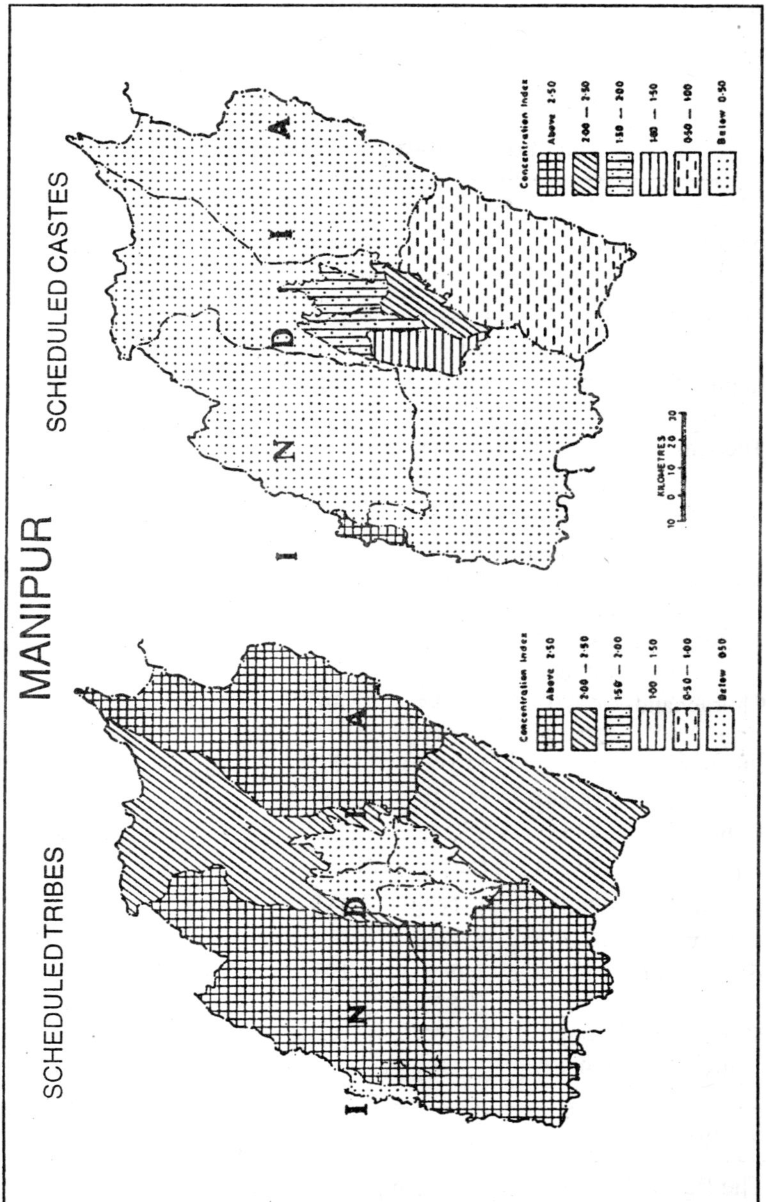
MANIPUR
SCHEDULED TRIBES
SCHEDULED CASTES
I N D I A
Concentration Index
Above 2·50
2·00 — 2·50
1·50 — 2·00
1·00 — 1·50
0·50 — 1·00
Below 0·50
KILOMETRES
10 0 10 20 30

Fig. 2.10

whereas Bishnupur and Thoubal districts have a little over one-third of their population residing in the towns (Fig. 2.8)

Table 2.10

Area and Population of Manipur, 1991

District/ Region	Area (km^2)	Population	Density (per km^2)	Percentage of urban Population	Growth Rate (1981-91)
Imphal East	673 (3.01)	330460 (17.98)	491	22.94	28.86
Imphal West	555 (2.49)	380801 (20.73)	686	56.69	27.06
Thoubal	514 (2.30)	293958 (16.00)	572	36.55	26.83
Bishnupur	496 (2.22)	180773 (9.84)	364	34.94	28.07
Senapati	3271 (14.65)	208406 (11.34)	64	-	34.09
Tamenglong	4391 (19.67)	86278 (4.70)	20	-	38.51
Churachand-pur	4570 (20.47)	176184 (9.59)	39	19.11	30.72
Chandel	3313 (14.84)	71014 (3.87)	21	13.62	25.81
Ukhrul	4544 (20.35)	109275 (5.95)	24	-	31.74
Manipur valley	2067 (9.26)	1151946 (62.70)	555	39.61	27.56
Barak basin	171 (0.77)	34046 (1.85)	199	17.53	27.81
Manipur hills	20089 (89.97)	651157 (35.45)	32	6.65	32.38
MANIPUR	22327	1837149	82	27.52	29.29

The figures in brackets represent percentage.

Source : Census of India 1991.

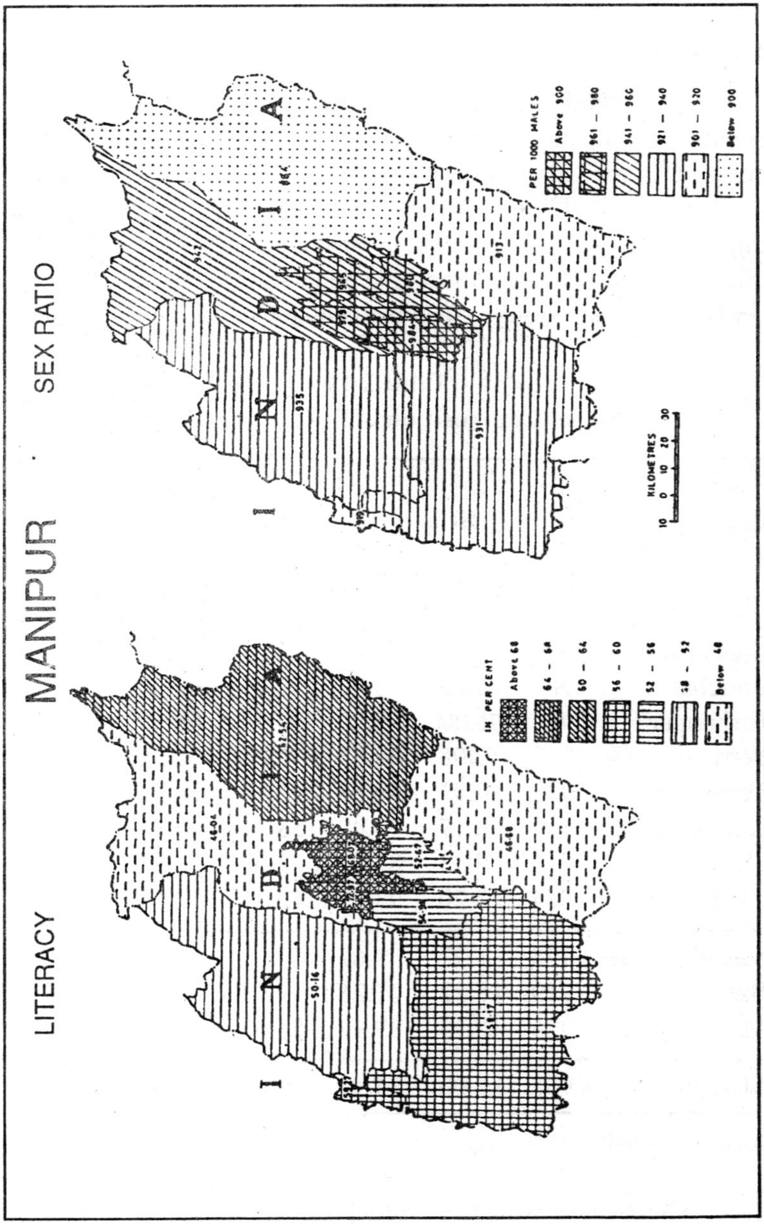
MANIPUR
LITERACY
SEX RATIO
IN PERCENT
PER 1000 MALES
KILOMETRES

Fig. 2.11

2.3.2 Social Composition ·

The scheduled castes constitute 2.02 per cent of state population with their largest concentration in the Barak basin, 18.32 per cent. In the valley districts their proportion ranges from 3.98 per cent in Imphal East to 3.76 per cent in Thoubal, 2.52 per cent in Imphal West and 1.29 per cent in Bishnupur district, while in the hill districts they form microscopic minority ranging between 0.04 per cent in Tamenglong to 0.33 per cent in Chandel (Table 2.11).

Table 2.11
Social Composition of Population 1991

District/ Region	Sex ratio	SC	ST	Percentage of Literacy		
				Persons	Males	Females
Imphal East	966	3.98	5.81	68.05	80.65	52.26
Imphal West	979	2.52	3.86	73.01	84.63	61.12
Thoubal	980	3.76	0.97	52.47	68.33	36.31
Bishnupur	984	1.29	5.30	54.94	68.59	41.13
Senapati	942	0.08	84.07	46.04	55.26	36.13
Tamenglong	935	0.04	96.58	50.16	59.92	39.67
Churachandpur	931	0.17	93.49	58.17	66.38	49.30
Chandel	913	0.33	85.52	46.68	57.39	34.80
Ukhrul	884	0.20	93.23	62.54	72.11	51.57
Manipur valley	978	1.73	3.69	64.01	77.91	50.75
Barak basin	919	18.32	11.26	59.27	69.96	47.50
Manipur hills	925	0.15	89.97	52.67	61.95	42.52
Manipur	958	2.02	34.41	59.89	71.63	47.60

Source : Census of India 1991.

The scheduled tribes, belonging to both Naga and Kuki groups, form 34.41 per cent of the state population. In the hill districts their population ratio ranges between 84.07 per cent in Senapati to 96.58 per cent in Tamenglong. In the valley districts they constitute 5.81 per cent of the population of Imphal East, 5.30 per cent of Bishnupur, 3.86 per cent of Imphal West's population and only 0.97 per cent of Thoubal's. Fig. 2.10 shows the concentration index of the scheduled caste and scheduled tribe population in the state.

The valley population comprise the Meiteis, the Pangals and the Nepalese. The Meiteis are mainly the Hindus and the Pangals-Muslims, both speaking Manipuri language, one of the national languages of the country. The Bengalis, Jains and Sikhs, Marwaris and Biharis live mainly in the towns and are engaged in trade and commerce and tertiary activities.

The sex ratio, females per thousand males, in Manipur is higher in the valley and lower in the hill districts, which ranges between 884 in Ukhrul to 984 in Bishnupur (Fig. 2.11). The literate persons constitute 59.89 per cent of state population as against 52.19 per cent for the country as a whole. Imphal West district registered the highest literacy, 73.01 per cent, and Senapati district the lowest, only 46.04 per cent. Except Imphal West, Imphal East and Ukhrul, all the districts recorded lower literacy than the state average (Fig. 2.11). The proportion of literates among the males (state average 71.63 per cent) ranges between 55.26 per cent in Senapati to 84.63 per cent in Imphal West. The female literacy (state average 47.60 per cent) too varied from 34.80 per cent in Chandel to 61.12 per cent in Imphal West district. Table 2.11 shows the pattern of literacy, both for males and females, at the district and regional level. The proportion of literates, both for males and females, is lower than the state average in all the districts except Imphal West, Imphal East and Ukhrul.

2.3.3 Occupational Pattern

Table 2.12 shows the number of workers (economically active population), comprising main workers and marginal workers, and

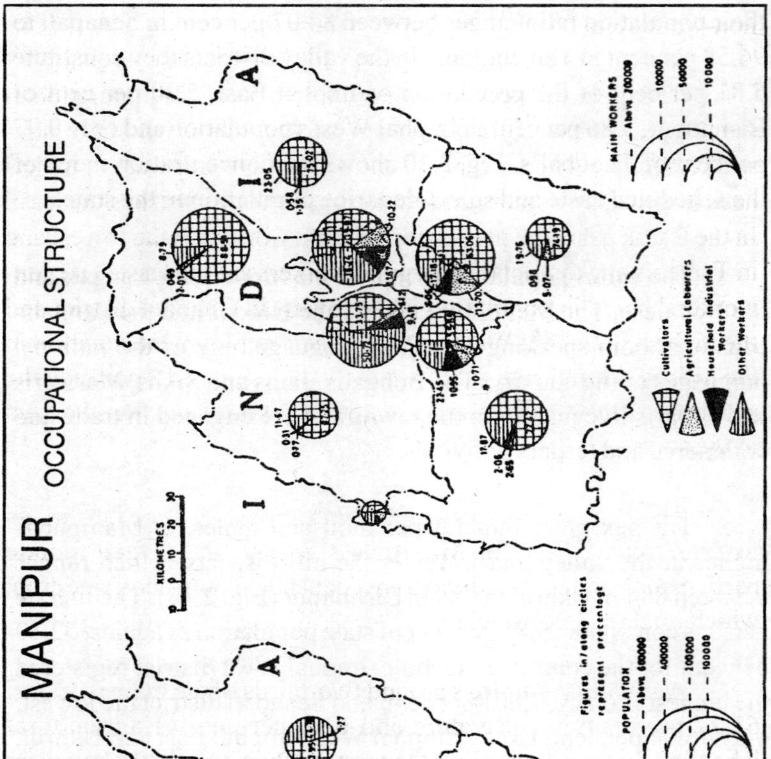
MANIPUR
WORKERS AND NON-WORKERS
OCCUPATIONAL STRUCTURE
KILOMETRES
POPULATION
Figures in/along circles represent percentage
Main Workers
Marginal Workers
Non-Workers
MAIN WORKERS
Cultivators
Agricultural Labourers
Household Industrial Workers
Other Workers

Fig. 2.12

non-workers in the state as per 1991 census.

The main workers constitute 38.55 per cent of population in the state and the marginal workers 3.63 per cent, while the non-workers form 57.82 per cent of state population. The valley districts have larger share of marginal workers and the hill districts the least. In the Barak basin the proportion of main workers is the lowest and in Tamenglong district the marginal workers are the least. The non-workers' share in population is the lowest in Chandel district and the highest in Imphal West district. Thus, employment situation in the hills is not so acute as it is in the valley. Fig. 2.12 portrays the proportion of the main workers, marginal workers and non-workers in the state.

The higher participation rate (the proportion of main workers to total population) in Manipur is due to the larger female participation and lopsided economy, dependent only upon rice crop, which is labour intensive.

Agriculture employs around two-thirds of the main workers, 61.77 per cent as cultivators and 6.69 per cent as agricultural labourers. In the hill districts, the proportion of agricultural workers is very high, ranging from 90.52 per cent in Senapati to 76.37 per cent in Ukhrul, while in Manipur valley it ranges between 76.76 per cent in Thoubal to 39.73 per cent in Imphal West. The percentage of cultivators is much larger in the hill districts and of agricultural labourers in the Barak basin and central valley. Workers in the secondary sector, in the household industries, constitute 11.62 per cent of the workforce in Imphal East and 10.95 per cent in Bishnupur districts, 9.44 per cent in Imphal West, 6.06 per cent in Thoubal and 2.06 per cent in Churachandpur district. In other districts in the Manipur hills, the share of household industry workers is less than one per cent. A large number of main workers are engaged in the tertiary sector, mainly the government services, and partly in transport and construction works.

Table 2.12
Workers and Non-Workers in Manipur, 1991

District/ Region	Workers		Non-workers
	Main workers	Marginal Workers	
(1)	(2)	(3)	(4)
Imphal East	106737	12019	211704
	(32.30)	(3.64)	(64.06)
Imphal West	122714	7882	250205
	(32.23)	(2.07)	(65.70)
Thoubal	107694	24547	161717
	(36.64)	(8.35)	(55.01)
Bishnupur	69114	11078	100581
	(38.23)	(6.13)	(55.64)
Senapati	104681	3439	100286
	(50.23)	(1.65)	(48.12)
Tamenglong	39210	494	46574
	(45.45)	(0.57)	(53.98)
Churachandpur	74899	2752	98533
	(42.51)	(1.56)	(55.93)
Chandel	34301	3022	33691
	(48.30)	(4.26)	(47.44)
Ukhrul	48933	1388	58954
	(44.78)	(1.27)	(53.95)
Manipur valley	395716	53783	702447
	(34.35)	(4.67)	(60.98)
Barak basin	10543	1743	21760
	(30.97)	(5.12)	(63.91)
Manipur hills	302024	11095	338038
	(46.38)	(1.70)	(51.92)
Manipur	708283	66621	1062246
	(38.55)	(3.63)	(57.82)

Figures in brackets represent percentage.

Source : Census of India 1991.

Table 2.13
Manipur : Occupational Structure, 1991

District/ Region	Cultiva-tors	Agricul-tural labourers	Household industry workers	Other workers
(1)	(2)	(3)	(4)	(5)
Imphal East	42473	11125	12404	40735
	(39.79)	(10.42)	(11.62)	(38.17)
Imphal West	41474	7278	11583	62379
	(33.80)	(5.93)	(9.44)	(50.83)
Thoubal	67916	14753	6527	18498
	(63.06)	(13.70)	(6.06)	(17.18)
Bishnupur	38627	7403	7565	15519
	(55.89)	(10.71)	(10.95)	(22.45)
Senapati	92652	2103	727	9191
	(88.51)	(2.01)	(0.69)	(8.79)
Tamenglong	34212	302	121	4575
	(87.25)	(0.77)	(0.31)	(11.67)
Churachandpur	57986	1988	1541	13384
	(77.42)	(2.65)	(2.06)	(17.87)
Chandel	25549	1739	337	6776
	(74.19)	(5.07)	(0.98)	(19.76)
Ukhrul	36710	659	284	11280
	(75.02)	(1.35)	(0.58)	(23.05)
Manipur valley	185871	38269	37608	133968
	(46.97)	(9.67)	(9.50)	(33.86)
Barak basin	4619	2290	471	3163
	(43.81)	(21.72)	(4.47)	(30.00)
Manipur hills	247009	6791	3010	45214
	(81.78)	(2.25)	(1.00)	(14.97)
Manipur	437499	47350	41089	182345
	(61.77)	(6.69)	(5.80)	(25.74)

Figures in brackets represent percentage of main workers.
Source : Census of India 1991.

The proportion of such workers, classed as other workers, varies from 8.79 per cent in Senapati district to 50.83 per cent in Imphal West district. Table 2.13 shows the proportion of main workers under industrial categories-cultivators, agricultural labourers, household industry workers and other workers in various districts and natural regions of the state. Fig. 2.12 depicts the occupational structure of population in Manipur at the district level.

2.3.4 Settlements

About three-fourths of the state population live in the villages of varied size and a little over one-fourth in the towns. Table 2.14 shows the blockwise distribution of villages and districtwise distribution of towns in Manipur according to their population size.

Table 2.14

Rural and Urban Settlements in Manipur

District/ Block/ Region	Population size of settlements							Total
	Below 200	200-500	500-1000	1000-2000	2000-5000	5000-10000	Above 10000	
Imphal East								
Rural	28	46	42	52	35	3	-	206
Urban	-	-	-	-	1	2	-	3
Porompat	5	3	7	13	18	2	-	48
Keirao Bitra	7	5	5	10	9	-	-	36
Sawombung	3	22	19	20	7	1	-	72
Jiribam	13	16	11	9	1	-	-	50
Imphal West								
Rural	8	19	30	30	29	1	-	117
Urban	-	-	-	-	2	5	3	10
Lamphelpat	-	-	1	1	8	1	-	11
Lamsang	7	11	19	4	5	-	-	46
Patsoi	1	2	4	14	7	-	-	28
Wangoi	-	6	6	11	9	-	-	32
Thoubal								
Rural	3	8	17	24	30	4	1	87
Urban	-	-	-	1	1	4	3	9
Thoubal	3	7	12	10	11	2	1	46
Lilong	-	-	3	7	7	-	-	17
Kakching	-	1	2	7	12	2	-	24
Bishnupur								
Rural	-	4	8	11	15	6	1	45
Urban	-	-	-	-	-	5	2	7
Bishnupur	-	-	3	3	9	-	-	15
Nambol	-	1	2	3	4	1	-	11

Moirang	-	3	3	5	2	5	1	19
Senapati								
Rural	263	149	58	29	16	1	-	516
Mao-Maram	10	21	17	11	6	-	-	65
Paomata	4	5	3	4	3	-	-	19
Purul	4	9	6	6	2	-	-	27
Saikul	129	70	8	1	-	-	-	208
Kangpokpi	25	19	15	6	4	1	-	70
Saitu	90	25	9	2	1	-	-	127
Tamenglong								
Rural	73	62	45	10	2	1	-	193
Tamei	2	12	12	4	-	-	-	30
Tousem	35	15	8	1	-	-	-	59
Tamenglong	13	17	12	3	-	1	-	46
Nungba	23	18	13	2	2	-	-	58
Churachandpur								
Rural	282	155	45	17	5	-	-	504
Urban	-	-	-	-	-	-	1	1
Parbung	8	16	13	3	2	-	-	42
Thanlon	14	24	5	3	1	-	-	47
Henglep	71	29	6	1	-	-	-	107
Samulamlan	68	16	2	2	-	-	-	88
Churachandpur	86	48	13	7	1	-	-	155
Singngat	35	22	6	1	1	-	-	65
Chandel								
Rural	179	91	21	1	-	-	-	292
Urban	-	-	-	-	-	1	-	1
Moreh	40	21	1	-	-	-	-	62
Machi	30	12	5	-	-	-	-	47
Chandel	47	27	8	-	-	-	-	82
Chakpikarong	62	31	7	1	-	-	-	101
Ukhrul								
Rural	88	68	44	18	3	-	1	222
Chingai	6	10	11	4	-	-	-	31
Ukhrul	8	17	21	14	3	-	1	64
Kasom Khullen	24	7	3	-	-	-	-	34
Kamjong	27	17	5	-	-	-	-	49
Phungyar-Phaisat	23	17	4	-	-	-	-	44
Manipur valley								
Rural	26	61	86	108	108	14	2	405
Urban	-	-	-	1	4	15	8	28
Barak basin								
Rural	13	16	11	9	1	-	-	50

Urban	-	-	-	-	-	1	-	1
Manipur hills								
Rural	885	515	213	75	26	2	1	1727
Urban	-	-	-	-	-	1	1	2
Manipur								
Rural	924	602	310	192	135	16	3	2182
Urban	-	-	-	1	4	17	9	31

Source : Census of India 1991.

Over four-fifths of the villages in the hill areas are too small, with population below 500. Such villages form about one-fifth of the rual settlements in the central valley and two-fifths in the Barak basin. Medium-sized villages, in the population range of 500-2000 constitute one-sixth of the hill villages, about half of the valley villages and two-fifths of the villages in the Barak basin. Large villages, with population above 2000, form less than two per cent of the hill villages, 30.62 per cent of the valley villages and two per cent of the villages in the Jiribam area.

Six blocks in the hill districts-Moreh, Machi and Chandel in Chandel district and Phungyar-Phaisat, Kamjong and Kasom Khullen in Ukhrul district lack villages with above 1000 population, while in Saikul block of Senapati and Tamei and Tousem blocks of Tamenglong all the villages are of small and medium size with population below 2000. Bishnupur district and Lilong and Kakching blocks of Thoubal district and Lamphelpat and Wangoi blocks of Imphal West district have no village with population below 200. Three villages-Khangabok (12925) in Thoubal block, Thanga (12386) in Moirang block and Ukhrul (10440) in Ukhrul block have population above 10000 persons.

Manipur valley has 28 towns including Imphal city (198535), the state capital, the Manipur hills two towns and the Barak basin one town. Out of 10 towns of Imphal West district, Imphal is a class I town (100000 and above), Mayang Imphal and Samurou Class IV towns (10000-19999), Thongkhong Laxmi Bazar, Lilong Chajing,

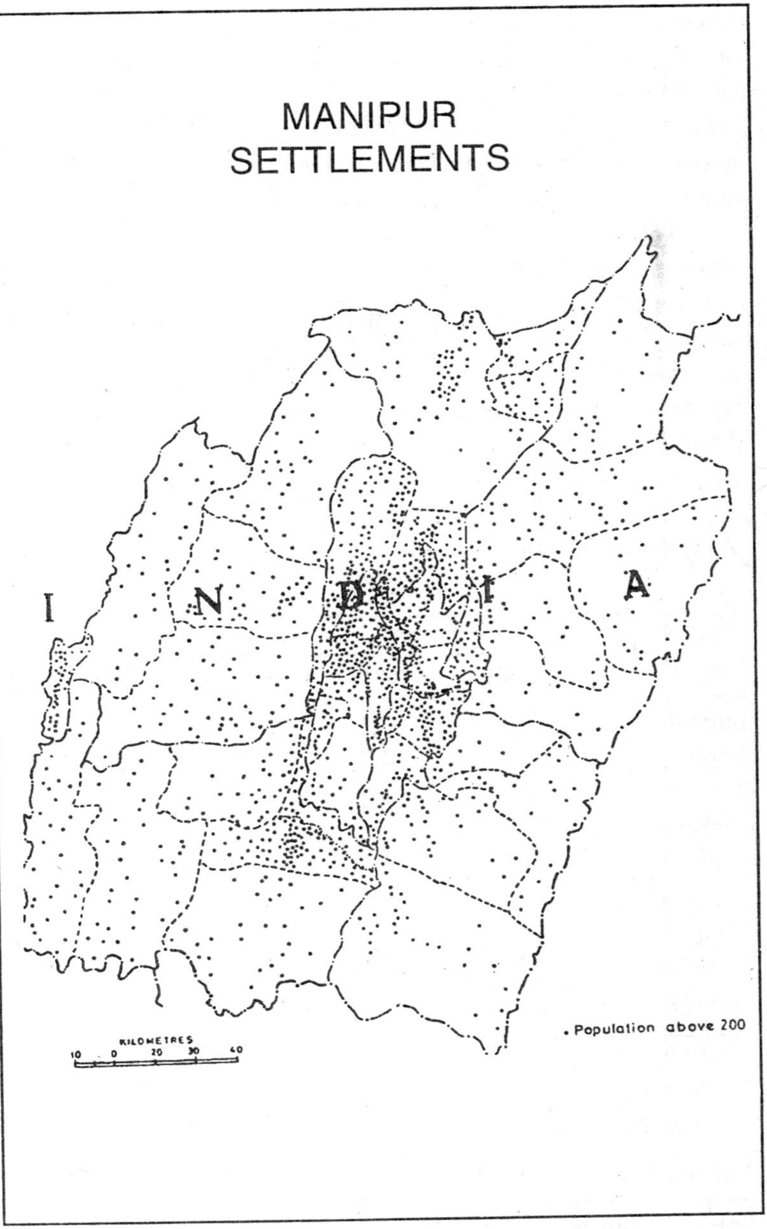
MANIPUR
SETTLEMENTS
I N D I A
. Population above 200
KILOMETRES
10 0 20 30 40

Fig. 2.13

Lamjaotongba, Wangoi and Lamsang Class V towns (5000-9999), and Sekmai Bazar and Bijoy Govinda class VI towns (Below 5000). In Thoubal district, out of nine towns, Thoubal and Kakching are class III towns (20000-49999), Lilong a class IV town, Kakching Khunou, Yairipok, Wangjing and Sikhong Sekmai class V towns, and Sugnu and Heirok class VI towns. In Bishnupur district, there are seven towns, of which Nambol and Moirang are class IV towns, and Ningthoukhong, Bishnupur, Kumbi, Oinam and Kwakta class V towns. In Imphal East district, Andro and Jiribam are class V towns, and Lamlai a class VI town.Churachandpur is a class III town and Moreh in Chandel district a class V town. Fig. 2.8 shows the size class of towns, while Fig. 2.13 portrays the spatial distribution of settlements in Manipur.

Table 2.15
Average Population Size and Area of Settlements in Manipur, 1991

District/	Villages		Towns	
Region	Population	Area (km^2)	Population	Area (km^2)
Imphal East	1236	3.17	21264	5.32
Imphal West	1409	4.29	22868	5.92
Thoubal	214	5.58	11939	3.18
Bishnupur	2613	10.20	9024	5.29
Senapati	404	6.34	-	-
Tamenglong	447	22.75	-	-
Churachandpur	283	9.05	33666	6.50
Chandel	210	11.34	9673	1.00
Ukhrul	492	20.46	-	-
Manipur valley	1717	4.76	16298	4.81
Barak basin	562	3.36	5969	3.20
Manipur hills	352	11.63	21669	3.75
Manipur	610	10.17	16311	4.69

Source : Census of India 1991.

There are wide variations in the average population size and areal extent of the villages and towns in various districts and ecological settings in the state. Table 2.15 shows the average population and area for the rural and urban settlements in Manipur.

The average population per village varies from 210 in Chandel district to 2613 in Bishnupur district, while the average area per village ranges between 3.17 km^2 in Imphal East district and 22.75 km^2 in Tamenglong district. The average population size of the towns is the smallest in Bishnupur district, only 9024 persons, and the largest in Churachandpur district, i.e. 33666 persons. Average area for the towns ranges between 1.00 km^2 in Chandel district and 6.50 km^2 in Churachandpur district.

2.3.4.1 Imphal City

Imphal (24°48'N/13°57'E), a cluster of homesteads built around Kangla the royal residency in the past, is the administrative, cultural and economic hub of the state. It is a well planned city spread over an area of 33.30 km^2 with well marked functional zones - the central business district comprising the Thangal, Paona and associated markets popularly known as the Khwairamband bazar, surrounded by educational, administrative, medical, industrial and recreational areas. Criss-crossed by rivers Imphal, Nambul, Naga and Kongba, which have roads on their embankments on either sides, the city faces flash floods during the rainy season. Langol, Chingmeirong, Chinga-Lalambung and Nongmeibung hills and hillocks provide the city scenic spots and healthy environ for its residents. Lamphelpat, once a swampy marsh on its north-western part, has now been reclaimed for residential, governmental institutional and agricultural purposes. Traversed by the National Highways 39, 53 and 150 and the state highways, the city is well connected with all the distinct and subdivisional headquarters, and the neighbouring state capitals, commercial centres and rail heads is Nagaland, Assam, Mizoram and Myanmar.

The city is divided into 26 municipal wards besides Kangla in the centre with well marked residential areas of Khwai, Khurai, Wangkhei and Yaiskul. It accomodates the state and central governement offices, a large number of educational and cultural institutions, banks and financial organisations, clubs and playgrounds besides the world famous Pologround, temples and the sports complex. Imphal, which had a population of 1,98,535 in 1991, and its suburbs accommodate currently about one-sixth of the states population.

2.3.5 Social Facilities

The state, particularly its vast hilly tribal tract, suffers from want of adequate social facilities both in terms of quantity and quality. There are at present 2571 primary schools, 631 middle schools, 510 high schools, 72 higher secondary schools, 64 degree colleges, 4 professional colleges including Regional Institute of Medical Sciences (RIMS), one polytechnic, an engineering college, 19 technical and industrial schools and two universities Manipur and Central Agricultural University. The institutions, in general are poorly equipped with regard to infrastructure like building, staff, laboratory, playgrounds, etc.

Manipur has 69 primary health centres, 440 primary health sub-centres, 14 community health centres, 28 dispensaries and 28 hospitals with 2367 beds, the population served per bed being 776 persons. Postal and telecommunication facilities are inadequate as about three-fourths of the villages lack postal facilities and even all the towns have not been linked with telecommunication facilities.

Other facilities like banking, credit institutions, marketing, seed and fertilizer distribution centres, safe drinking water and rural electrification are also found inadequate in the state.

2.4 Conclusion

It is apparent from the above outline that the state, although possessing abundant forest, soil, water and human resources, exhibits prominently the features of a depressed economy-over population in the central valley, high rate of population growth, predominance of primary activities, low productivity in agriculture, high degree of unemployment, overwhelmingly rural tribal folk. particularly in the hills, steeped into conventional outlook, lack of basic amenities and infrastructure and all these leading to an ever-accelerating vicious cirecle of poverty.

Ever-increasing population, poor economic growth and rampant unemployment have to be checked by effective planning of this resource rich state which is currently witnessing social upheavals for the lack of initiatives and programmes for its socio-economic transformation. For evolving a strategy for an integrated development of Manipur attempts have been made to identify the basic planning units and their service/growth centres in the succeeding parts of this study.

3

Growth Centres and Planning Regions

The process of integrated regional development primarily rests upon two types of integration-spatial and functional, which are themselves interrelated. Functional integration of various sectors such as agriculture, horticulture, industry, infrastructure, etc. has to be taken up by making use of a spatial model, in which development in one sector opens up possibilities for the development in another. The spatial relationship among various socio-economic activities depend a great deal on where they are located. It is observed that activities often cluster in hierarchical pattern in space. The existing hierarchic linkages between central places and their service areas based on their functional relationships are used for contemplating the optimum utilisation of new investments as well as for decentralisation of developmental activities down to the grassroot level in order to conceive an overall and all-round development of the region.

The spatial model used for these two levels of integration is based on carefully selected basic units of planning at various hierarchic levels, which is based on the fact that development in a region does not take place without any pattern, rather the space is organised in a definite system. This concept has been expressed in the theory of growth centre planning-a modified form of the basic theories of J.H. Von Thunen (1826), Walter Christaller (1933) and August Losch (1954), which was later expanded by Francois Perroux (1955), B.J.L. Berry (1958) and J.R. Boudville (1966), etc. The first task in a growth centre planning has, therefore, been to identify the focal points of growth which will be centrally located within their service areas and will be functionally linked with the dependent settlements for various activities. To identify such a hierarchy of these centres of growth and delineation of their respective hinterlands, considered here as basic planning units, is the main focus of this part of the study.

3.1 Identification of Growth Centres

The focal points of growth-the growth centres, growth points and service centres in the present context, form a nested hierarchy of central places, and their complementary regions or service areas appropriate units of planning. In an integrated spatio-sectoral development of a region, these central places assume an effective role in containing the polarisation process and speeding up the spread effects in space economy.

3.1.1 Central Place System

Central places constitute a system that has a spatial expression on the landscape. A central place is like a gravity centre which depicts the maximum interaction of people. The term central place was first used by M. Jefferson (1931) for a focus of manifold human activities which provide the services to its surrounding region that gives it a certain degree of importance in relation to other places.

The central place system forms a hierarchical geographical arrangement, with centres linked to larger ones in a variety of ways:

a. The larger the central place, the greater the variety of central functions.

b. The larger the central place, the greater the distance to a place of comparable size. Places at the upper end of the hierarchy are widely spaced whereas smaller centres are much closely packed together.

c. Places at the same level in the hierarchy offer the same mix of tertiary goods and services. They also offer the same set of functions found in lower order centres, and

d. The higher the level in the hierarchy, the lower the number of central places at that level. There are, then, numerous lower order places, several intermediate order places, and only a few higher order central places.

The magnitude of the surplus of goods, services or functions offered by a place to its tributary area is attributed to be the centrality of any place.

3.1.2 Centrality

Centrality is the relative importance of a place with regard to the region surrounding it. The concept of centrality implies the extent, number, size, quality and quantity of the goods and services provided by the central place to its hinterland or trade area.

The centrality of a place can be measured to determine its central place status. Various methods have been evolved to measure the centrality. The commonly used methods are based on assumption that higher the level of service functions and functional hierarchy, higher will be the centrality of places. The concept of centrality, when applied to predominantly rural area, such as Manipur hills, has to take note of, among other things, the population size of the settlements, which often serves as a proxy variable for many existing functions. This is because larger the population, greater is the demand for services and functions and greater is the pull of the places to attract them over time.

According to John E. Brush and H.E. Bracey (1967) the importance of a centre or its centrality can be assessed in two ways : (i) measurement of the business activities and other services existing in the centre, and (ii) determination of the area dependent upon the centre for goods and services. Commerce, therefore, is the most uniformly and ubiquitously diffused central place function through the various grades of service centres, small and large, whose functional development owes essentially to the provision of goods and services to the rural population (Kashi N. Singh, 1966).

Edward L. Ullman (1941) suggested that if one knew the average number of customers required to support certain specialised functions in various regions, then the excess of these functions over the normal required for the urban population would be an index of centrality. As such, a centre having more commercial population than another centre of equal size is more significant as a central place.

The average commercial population in Manipur is 3.83 per cent with large disparities in its spatial distribution (Fig. 3.1). In the central valley Imphal West district has the largest proportion of workers in trade and commerce, 10.01 per cent as against 5.83 per cent in Imphal East, 2.87 per cent in Bishnupur and 2.02 per cent in Thoubal district. Among the hill districts, Chandel has 4.55 per cent of the commercial population, Churachandpur 1.59 per cent and Ukhrul 1.14 per cent. Senapati and Tamenglong districts have a meagre ratio of workers in commercial activity, only 0.83 and 0.82 per cent respectively. Jiribam in Barak basin has an impressive proportion of commercial population (5.04 per cent) (Table 3.1).

Table 3.1

Commercial and Non-agricultural Population 1991

(in per cent)

District	Commercial Population	Non-Agricultural Population
Imphal East	5.83	51.46
Imphal West	10.01	60.27
Thoubal	2.02	23.24
Bishnupur	2.87	33.40
Senapati	0.83	9.48
Tamenglong	0.82	11.98
Churachandpur	1.59	19.93
Chandel	4.55	20.75
Ukhrul	1.14	23.63
Jiribam	5.04	34.47
Manipur	3.83	31.55

Source : Census of India, 1991.

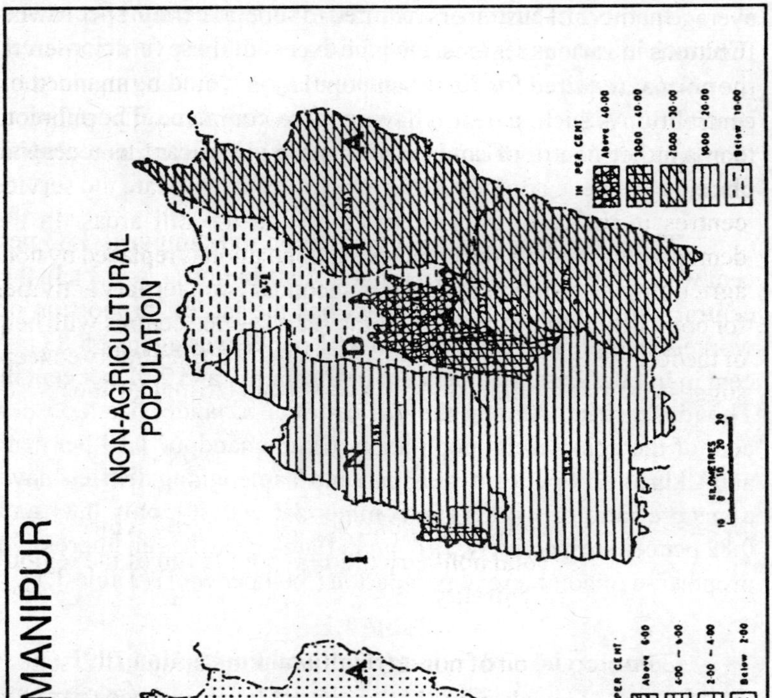
MANIPUR
COMMERCIAL POPULATION
NON-AGRICULTURAL POPULATION
IN PER CENT
Above 6.00
4.00 – 6.00
2.00 – 4.00
Below 2.00
IN PER CENT
Above 40.00
30.00 – 40.00
20.00 – 30.00
10.00 – 20.00
Below 10.00
KILOMETRES
I N D I A
I N D I A

Fig. 3.1

In the hill areas of the state, there are only two towns-Churachandpur and Moreh, which have impressive commercial population, but the villages numbering 1727, ranging in their population size from 4 to 10440, lack in commerce. Therefore, to cover up the functional and spatial gaps in the region, demographic method has been adopted in the present study to locate the service centres in the rural tracts, particularly in the hill areas. In the demographic method, the commercial population is replaced by non-agricultural population engaged in secondary and tertiary activities for computing centrality score of the rural service centres with help of the following formula-a modified version of the centrality concept suggested by S. Godlund (1956) and Kashi N. Singh (1966) :

$$C = \frac{N.\ 100}{P}$$

Where N = Non-agricultural population of the centre
P = Total non-agriculutural population of the region
C = Centrality

The proportion of non-agricultural population in the state is 31.55 per cent (Table 3.1). At the district level, it ranges between 9.48 per cent in Senapati and 60.27 per cent in Imphal West. Hill districts, in general, have smaller numbers of non-agricultual workers than the valley districts (Fig. 3.1).

Though centrality score provides an effective measure of the degree of centrality of a central place, it does not take into account the institutional and administrative service functions- the functional establishments, which decide the nature and quality of higher order central places-the growth points and growth centres.

3.1.3 Functional Establishments

The service functions, both institutional and administrative or policy oriented, tend to correspond to the administrative status of a centre. Most of the policy functions are concentrated at the district, subdivisional and block headquarters which serve as nucleus for

MANIPUR
HIERARCHY OF CENTRAL PLACES
L - Lamphelpat
P - Porompat
23 Ngaikhong Khullen
24 Hoareibi
25 Irong Chaisaba
26 Maijing
27 Leisangthem
28 Hiyanglam
29 Heirok
30 Sugnu
31 Samulamlan
32 Keirap Kunthak
1 Irpisemba
2 Naorem Pakhanglakpa
3 Mengsangei
4 Hiyangthang
5 Kodompokpi
6 Samurou
7 Lilong Chajing
8 Mayang Imphal
9 Tulihal
10 Changamdabi
11 Thongju
12 Kshetrigao
13 Heingang
14 Koirengei
15 Khonghampat
16 Mayang Langjing
17 Phayang
18 Lamjaotongba
19 Uitou
20 Leimapokpam
21 Oinam
22 Irengbam
KILOMETRES
10 0 10 20 30
GROWTH CENTRES
GROWTH POINTS
SERVICE CENTRES
Jessami
Senapati
Ukhrul
Tamenglong
Jiribam
IMPHAL
Bishnupur
Thoubal
Churachandpur
Chandel
MOREH
TOUSEM
TADUBI
KANGPOKPI
SAIKUL
KAMJONG
NUNGBA
HENGLEP
MOIRANG
KAKCHING
THANLON
SINGNGAT
PARBUNG
CHAKPIKARONG
CHINGAI
PHUNGYAR
KASOM KHULLEN
MACHI
SAWOMBUNG
PAOMATA
PURUL
TAMEI

Fig. 3.2

developmental activities. The district headquarters with higher level adminstrative, health, educational, transport, communication and financial institutions/facilities/establishments exert a strong influence over their surroundings encompassing the entire district. Similarly, the sub-divisional/block headquarters with their developmental infrastructure and institutions generate growth impulses over their entire service area.

The functional establishments at the district and block headquarters are not only important in themselves as attributes of central places but also serve as nucleus for crystallizing commercial and tertiary functions around them. In the present study, therefore, nine district headquarters-Imphal East (Porompat), Imphal West (Lamphelpat), Thoubal, Bishnupur, Senapati, Tamenglong, Churachandpur, Chandel and Ukhrul besides Jiribam, a block headquarters on the western outskirts of the state with most of the district-level institutions and infrastructure, have been identified as growth centres, and all the subdivisional/block headquarters as growth points (Fig. 3.2), mainly for their policy functions.

3.1.4 Hierarchy of Central Places

The central places, identified on the basis of their functional establishments and centrality scores arrived at with the help of their non-agricultural population, revealing their qualitative and quantitative characteristics, form a three-tier hieracrhy composed of 10 first order, 39 second order and 189 third order central places designated as growth centres, growth points and service centres respectively in the present study. Fig. 3.2 depicts the hierarchy of central places in Manipur, details of which have been furnished in Table 3.2.

On an average, there are 3.90 growth points for each growth centre and 4.85 service centres in the hinterland of each growth point. The districtwise distribution of central places in Manipur (Table 3.3) shows that the maximum number of central places to the total settlements are found in the central valley district of

Bishnupur and the minimum in the northern hill district of Senapati. Thus, larger the number of settlements, smaller is the proportion of central places.

Table. 3.2

Hierarchy of Central Places in Manipur

Growth Centre	Growth Point	Service Centres
1	2	3
Imphal East	Porompat	Thongju, Kshetrigao, Heingang, Koirengei
	Keirao Bitra	Tulihal, Andro, Changamdabi, Moirang Purel
	Sawombung	Lamlai, Chingangbam, Sagolmang, Khundrakpam, Laikot
Imphal West	Lamphelpat	Iroisemba, Naoriya Pakhanglakpa
	Lamsang	Sekmai, Kanglatongbi, Khonghampat, Phayeng, Mayang Langjing
	Patsoi	Konthoujam, Lamjaotongba, Maisnam Kangmong, Maklang
	Wangoi	Mayang Imphal, Lilong Chajing, Samurou, Mongsangei Hiyangthang, Kodompokpi
Thoubal	Thoubal	Khongjom, Heirok, Yairipok, Sikhong Sekmai, Wangjing
	Lilong	Haoreibi, Leisangthem, Moijing, Irong Chesaba
	Kakching	Kakching Khunou, Wabgai, Sugnu, Hiyanglam, Waikhong, Pallel
Bishnupur	Bishnupur	Nachou, Ningthoukhong, Ngaikhong Khullen, Phubala, Keinou

Table 3.2 (*Contd.*)

1	2	3
	Nambol	Oinam, Utlou, Leimapokpam, Irengbam
	Moirang	Thanga, Kwakta, Kumbi, Wangoo Ahallup, Saiton
Senapati	Tadubi	Makhan Centre, Punanamei, Mao Songsong, Tinsong, Yangkhullen, Maram Centre
	Paomata	Tunggam Khullen, Liyai Khullen, Laii
	Purul	Oinam, Phaibung Khullen, Khongdei Khuman, Thingba Khunou
	Saikul	Laikoiching, Thangal Surung, Leitanpokpi, Thangkangphai, Phunam Maring
	Kangpokpi	Keithalmanbi, Kalapahar, Chalwa
	Saitu	Motbung, Leimakhong, Kangchup
Tameng-long	Tousem	Old Magulong, Thiulon, Oinamlong, Namtiram
	Tamenglong	Marangjing, Akhui, Haochong, Shongphel Khunou, Awangkhul
	Tamei	Langmei, Kadi, Lenglong, Chaton, Lenta
	Nungba	Khoupum Chingthak. Noney, Dolang, Lubanglong, Nungnang
Churach-andpur	Parbung	Senvon, Pherzawl, Tinsuong, Patpuimun, Tipaimukh, Sibapurikhal
	Thanlon	Bukpi, Mualnuam, Suangsong, Leijangphai, Kaihlam
	Henglep	Santing, Charoi Khullen, Vungbuk, S. Nabil, Lhengjang
	Samulamlan	Sagang, Ngariyan, Keriap Khunthak,

Table 3.2 (*Contd.*)

1	2	3
		Khoirentak Khunou
	Churachandpur	Saikot, Mata, Thingkangphai, Teiseng, Lhangbung (Geljang), Gangpimaul
	Singngat	Behiang, Suvangdoh, Kangkap, Muallum, Lungchin
Chandel	Moreh	Tengnoupal, Narum, Aimol Khullen, Leibi, Chalsam Tengnoupal
	Machi	Lamlong Khullen, Tollen, Khoibu, Kangshang
	Chandel	Lambung, Liwa Khullen, Khudei Khunou, Komlathabi, Larong, Tonsen Khullen
	Chakpikarong	Khunbung Khunou, New Somtal, Molcham, Sugnu Lamhang, Khongkang Sawompa, Haika
Ukhrul	Chingai	Chingjaroi Christian, Paoyi, Jessami, Kharasom, New Tusom, Paorei
	Ukhrul	Hundung, Tolloi, Tuinem, Sanakeithal, Khamasom, Mapum
	Kasom Khullen	Nambashi, Mawai, Khamlang, Nongdam, Kangkuk
	Kamjong	Ningthi, Chatrik Khullen, Grihang, Maku, Nampisha, Chamu
	Phungyar	Thawai, Sekibung, Lungphu, Chadong, Sorbung, Phalang
Jiribam	Jiribam	Hilghat, Latingkhal, Jakuradhor, Sonapur, Borobekra, Boroikhal

Source : Centrality of settlements based on non- agricultural population, Census of India 1991. Details of the centrality score are shown in the Appendix.

Table 3.3
Distribution of Central Places in Manipur

District/ Region	Total settle ments	Total central places	Occurrence of classified central places		
			I Order	II Order	III Order
Imphal East	209 (9.44)	25 (11.96)	2 (8.00)	4 (16.00)	19 (76.00)
Imphal West	127 (5.74)	22 (17.32)	1 (4.55)	4 (18.18)	17 (77.27)
Thoubal	96 (4.34)	19 (19.79)	1 (5.26)	3 (15.79)	15 (78.95)
Bishnupur	52 (2.35)	18 (34.62)	1 (5.55)	3 (16.67)	14 (77.78)
Senapati	516 (23.32)	31 (6.01)	1 (3.23)	6 (19.35)	24 (77.42)
Tamenglong	193 (8.72)	24 (12.44)	1 (4.17)	4 (16.67)	19 (79.16)
Churachand-pur	505 (22.82)	38 (7.52)	1 (2.63)	6 (15.79)	31 (81.58)
Chandel	293 (13.24)	26 (8.87)	1 (3.84)	4 (15.38)	21 (80.78)
Ukhrul	222 (10.03)	35 (15.77)	1 (2.86)	5 (14.28)	29 (82.86)
Manipur valley	433 (19.57)	76 (17.55)	4 (5.26)	13 (17.11)	59 (77.63)
Manipur hills	1729 (78.13)	154 (8.91)	5 (3.25)	25 (16.23)	124 (80.52)
Barak basin	51 (2.30)	8 (15.69)	1 (12.50)	1 (12.50)	6 (75.00)
Manipur	2213 (100.00)	238 (10.75)	10 (4.20)	39 (16.39)	189 (79.41)

Figures in brackets refer to marginal total percentage.
Source : Appendix.

Only one-seventh of the central places are the towns and the rest six-sevenths rural centres. Most of the workforce in the towns is engaged in tertiary activities, mainly services, trade and commerce and in the rural centres in agriculture and cottage industries.

The agricultural workers form major chunk of the labour force in the central places with smaller population while in the larger central places the workforce is engaged mostly in the services, trade and commerce. Population size, functional set up of the workforce-agricultural and non-agricultural and the centrality score of the central places have been presented in the Appendix.

3.1.4.1 Growth Centres

A growth centre is of innovative and generative character with well developed administrative functions tending secondary and tertiary activities in the centre rienforcing its growth potential. In the growth centres are located the propulsive firms/industries/ establishments which exert growth impulses in their entire trade zone/hinterland. As identified earlier, there are ten growth centres in the state which exhibit the functional units of retail shopping and wholesale distribution, commercial banks, industrial estate/ establishments, institutions of higher education, post and telegraph offices, district hospital, district rural development agency and district headquarters. National and State Highways connect the growth centres with the state capital-Imphal.

3.1.4.2 Growth Points

All the second order central places, which are block/ subdivisional headquarters, have been identified as growth points which provide developmental infrastructure to their trade/service areas through the block development offices. The main functional units found among growth points are retail shops, cooperative banks/ cooperative credit societies, higher secondary schools/colleges, sub-post offices, primary health centres/hospitals and facilities for vocational/extension training and services. State Highways and district roads form the transport network connecting the growth points with the growth centres, while the district and inter-village roads connect them with service centres in their hinterland. The growth points exhibit the characteristics of sub-regional innovative and propulsive centres which handle and process the agricultural and other products of their hinterland. These functions at growth points would lead to social and economic integration in sub-regions served by them.

3.1.4.3 Service Centres

The third order central places, designated as service centres, serve a rural population of 2900 to 8600 in the hill districts and 8400 to 12400 in the valley districts. Table 3.4 shows the area and population served by the service centres under different growth centres of the state.

Table 3.4
Area and Population under Service Centres

Growth Centre	No. of service centres	Service Area (km²)	Population served (1991)
Imphal East	13	34.58	11924
Imphal West	17	29.35	9702
Thoubal	15	32.36	12434
Bishnupur	14	32.79	8400
Senapati	24	136.29	8684
Tamenglong	19	231.11	4541
Churachandpur	31	147.21	4597
Chandel	21	157.71	2921
Ukhrul	29	156.69	3766
Jiribam	6	27.97	4680
Manipur	189	117.36	7045

Source : Census of India 1991.

The functions of the service centres include education up to high school in the hills and college level in the valley,branch or sub post offices, primary health centres/sub-centres, lower order development services through village level workers, cooperative societies, small markets with few shops/vendors, clubs and recreational facilities. Linked by inter-village roads, mostly unmetalled in the hills, these centres act as focal points for social intercourse and diffusion of developmental information to the villages and hamlets in their complementary area.

The hinterlands or service areas of the central places provide appropriate spatial units for developmental planning of the state.

3.2 Delimitation of Planning Regions

The hinterlands or the service areas of the central places-growth centres, growth points and service centres form different levels of planning units determining the functional relationship between the central places and their dependent settlements.

The service areas of the growth centres and growth points have been delineated on the basis of district and block boundaries (Fig. 3.3), and that of the service centres on the basis of William J. Reilly's Retail Gravitational Model (1931) :

$$\frac{T_a}{T_b} = \frac{P_a}{P_b}\left(\frac{d_b}{d_c}\right)$$

Where T_a and T_b are the trade to cities a and b

P_a and P_b are the population of a and b

d_a and d_b are the distances from the place being considered to cities a and b.

Two service centres, thus, attract trade from an intermediate settlement in the vicinity of the breaking point (the boundary between their hinterlands) approximately in direct proportion to the population of the two service centres and in inverse proportion to the squares

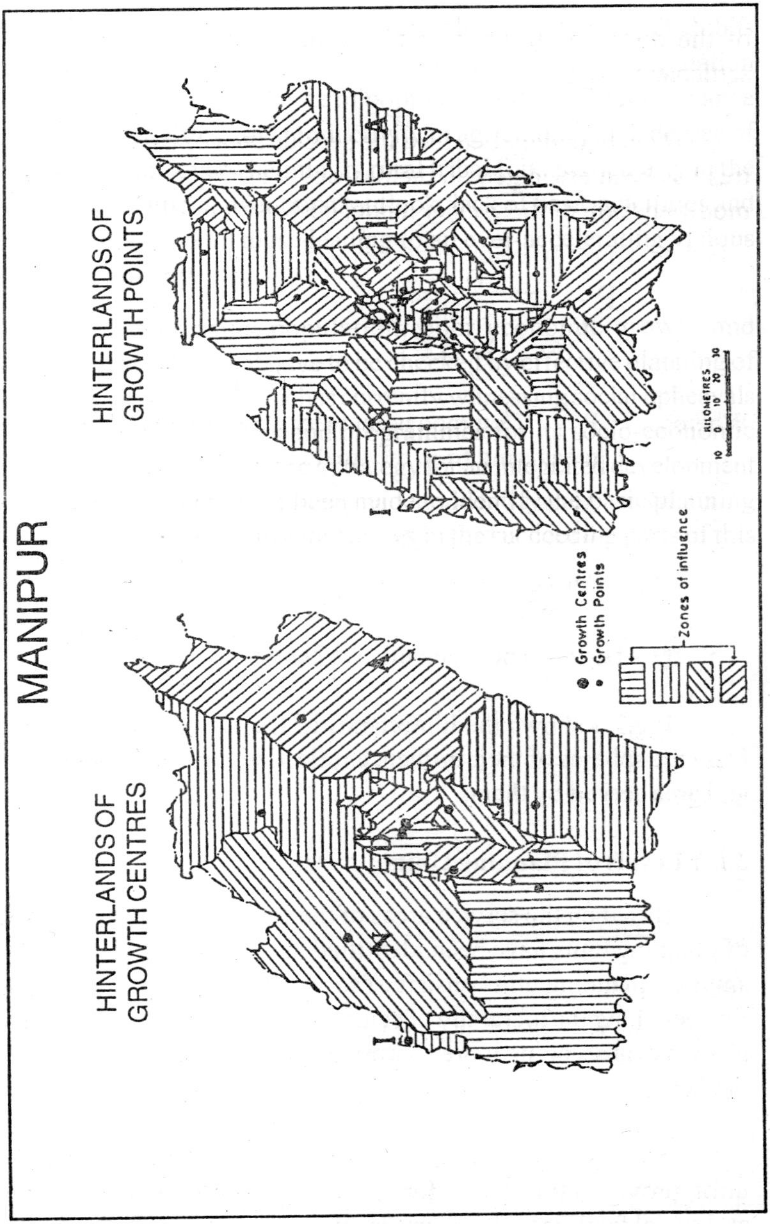
MANIPUR
HINTERLANDS OF GROWTH CENTRES
HINTERLANDS OF GROWTH POINTS
Growth Centres
Growth Points
Zones of influence
KILOMETRES
10 0 10 20 30

Fig. 3.3

of the distances from these two central places to intermediate settlement.

The boundary between the service area of two service centres has been estimated on the basis of breaking point equation, a modified form of the gravity model (G.Rushton, 1972) :

$$P = \frac{D}{1+\sqrt{\frac{M_a}{M_b}}}$$

Where P = Common point where the two hinterlands meet, measuring from the smaller centre

M_a = Mass of centre a measured by population size, which is bigger of the two centres

M_b = Mass of centre b measured by population size, which is smaller of the two centres

D = Distance between the two centres.

Fig.3.4 shows the hinterlands of the service centres which form the spheres of their influence reflecting the size of population and area served by them.

3.2.1 Levels of Planning Units

Based on the service areas of the central places, three levels of planning units have been identified in the state (Table 3.5). The smallest planning unit consists of service centre and its hinterland. Further along the hierarchy of central places, the growth points and growth centres being more central in character, have larger hinterlands and accordingly larger planning units (Fig. 3.5).

The service centre hinterlands, forming the basic planning units, provide a framework for designing agricultural infrastructure and social facilities. These first-level units provide optimum territorial expanse for the provisions of agricultural depots selling agri-

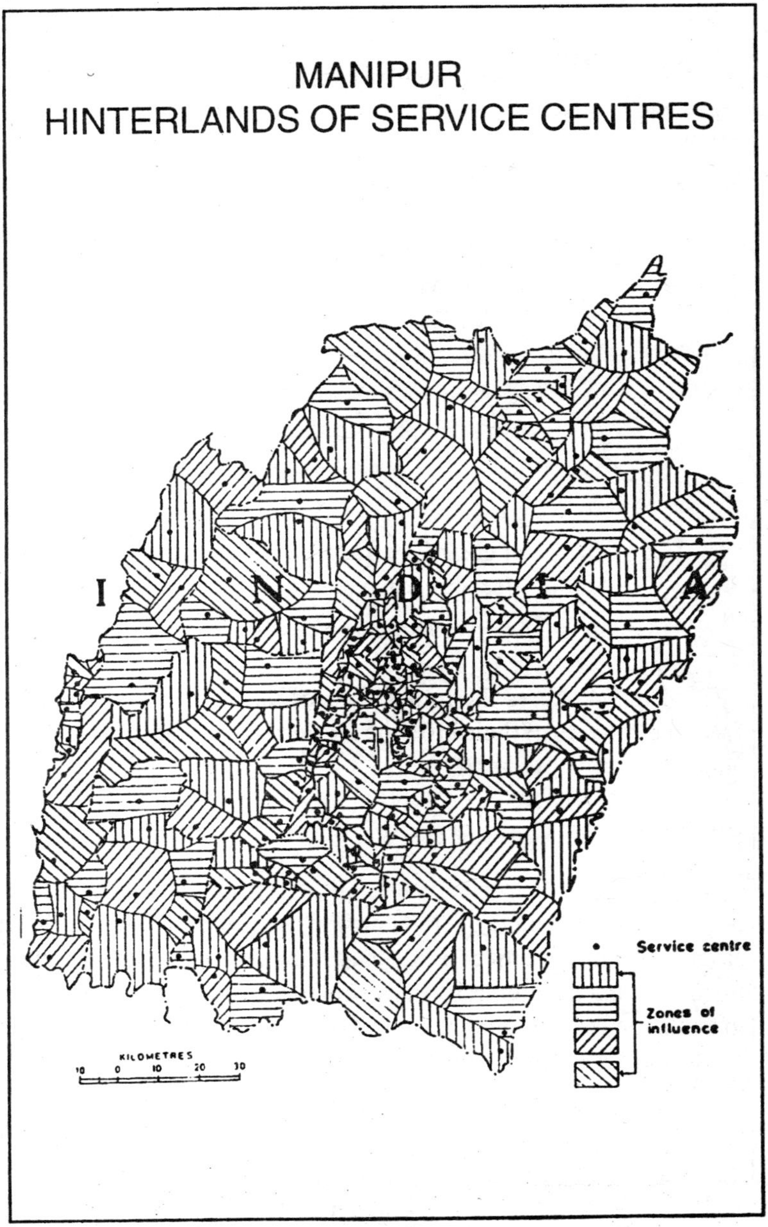
MANIPUR
HINTERLANDS OF SERVICE CENTRES
I N D I A
Service centre
Zones of influence
KILOMETRES
10 0 10 20 30

Fig. 3.4

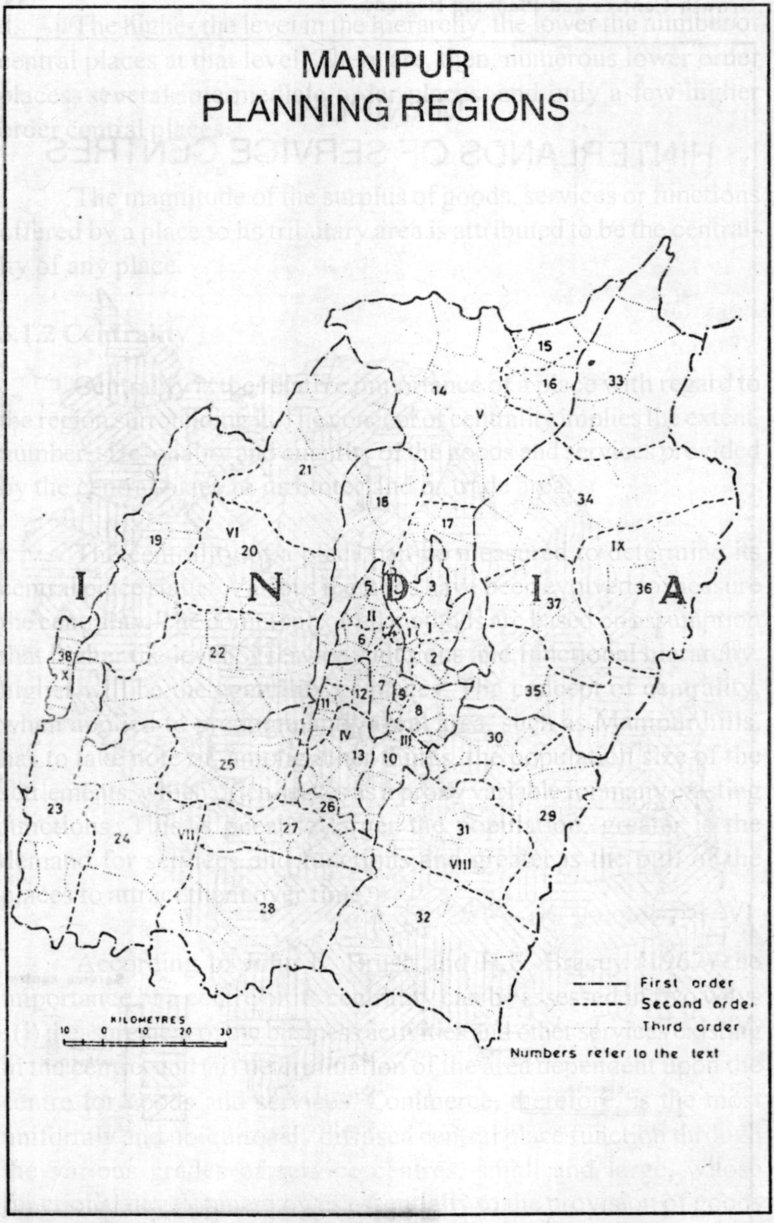
MANIPUR
PLANNING REGIONS
I N D I A
First order
Second order
Third order
Numbers refer to the text
KILOMETRES
10 0 10 20 30

Fig. 3.5

cultural inputs-seeds, fertilisers, insecticides and pesticides, and farm equipments, and handling farm produces purchased from the farmers at remunerative prices, schools for the children and medical and health care facilites for the sick so that the people need not travel long distances to avail of these facilities.

Table 3.5
Planning Regions in Manipur

First Order (Planning regions)	Second Order (Planning sub-regions)	Third Order (Basic planning units)-Number
(1)	(2)	(3)
I. Imphal East Region	1. Porompat region	4
	2. Keirao Bitra region	4
	3. Sawombung region	5
II. Imphal West Region	4. Lamphelpat region	2
	5. Lamsang region	5
	6. Patsoi region	4
	7. Wangoi region	6
III. Thoubal Region	8. Thoubal region	5
	9. Lilong region	4
	10. Kakching region	6
IV. Bishnupur Region	11. Bishnupur region	5
	12. Nambol region	4
	13. Moirang region	5
V. Senapati Region	14. Mao-Maram region	6
	15. Paomata region	3
	16. Purul region	4
	17. Saikul region	5
	18. Kangpokpi region	3
	19. Saitu region	3
VI. Tamenglong Region	20. Tousem region	4

(1)	(2)	(3)
	21. Tamenglong region	5
	22. Tamei region	5
	23. Nungba region	5
VII. Churachandpur Region	24. Parbung region	6
	25. Thanlon region	5
	26. Henglep region	5
	27. Samulamlan region	4
	28. Churachandpur region	6
	29. Singngat region	5
VIII. Chandel Region	30. Moreh region	5
	31. Machi region	4
	32. Chandel region	6
	33. Chakpikarong region	5
IX. Ukhrul Region	34. Chingai region	6
	35. Ukhrul region	6
	36. Kasom Khullen region	5
	37. Kamjong region	6
	38. Phungyar region	6
X. Jiribam region	39. Jiribam region	6

Source : Appendix.

The hinterlands of the growth points, forming second level planning units designated as planning sub-regions, provide spatial dimension for developing higher order functions and infrastructure such as agricultural extension services, cooperative banks and credit societies, primary health centres and dispensaries, secondary schools and colleges, and regulated markets.

The growth centre hinterlands constitute the third level planning units, termed as planning regions in the present study, which provide ideal territorial units for the development of industries and higher social facilities and infrastructure-institutions of higher learning, hospitals and clinics, commercial banks and financial institutions, wholesale and retail markets, transport, communication, water supply and irrigation, etc.

Table 3.6
Functional Characteristics of Planning Regions

Planning Region/ Sub-region	Population	% of			% of Main Workers as	
		Main workers	Marginal workers	Non workers	Agricul-tural workers	Non-agri-cultural workers
(1)	(2)	(3)	(4)	(5)	(6)	(7)
Imphal East	296414	32.45	3.47	64.08	48.54	51.46
Porompat	160666	28.01	3.96	67.96	32.08	67.92
Keirao Bitra	55233	37.15	2.45	60.40	61.44	38.56
Sawombung	80515	37.98	3.17	58.85	64.67	35.33
Imphal West	380801	32.23	2.07	65.70	39.73	60.27
Lamphelpat	176695	28.31	1.01	70.68	3.87	96.13
Lamsang	47375	38.56	3.02	58.42	74.99	25.01
Patsoi	56948	36.80	1.97	61.23	62.20	37.80
Wangoi	99783	33.36	3.57	63.07	54.96	45.04
Thoubal	293958	36.63	8.35	55.02	76.76	23.24
Thoubal	139866	37.48	9.25	53.27	76.26	23.74
Lilong	53834	31.48	9.99	58.53	74.53	25.47

(1)	(2)	(3)	(4)	(5)	(6)	(7)
Kakching	100258	35.44	6.15	58.41	78.54	21.46
Bishnupur	180773	38.23	6.13	55.64	66.60	33.40
Bishnupur	51844	37.93	6.44	55.63	61.54	38.46
Nambol	39943	40.18	4.26	55.56	66.41	33.59
Moirang	88986	37.53	6.79	55.68	69.67	30.33
Senapati	208406	50.23	1.65	48.12	90.52	9.48
Mao-Maram	49676	60.09	1.35	38.56	87.87	12.13
Paomata	19448	56.20	0.51	43.29	92.92	7.08
Purul	22213	51.45	2.55	46.00	96.28	3.72
Saikul	40069	49.40	0.89	49.71	91.96	8.04
Kangpokpi	48244	43.42	2.55	54.03	90.05	9.95
Saitu	28756	40.79	1.80	57.41	80.79	19.21
Tamenglong	86278	45.45	0.57	53.98	88.02	11.98
Tousem	15928	48.90	1.10	50.00	95.09	4.91
Tamenglong	27225	43.96	0.15	55.89	78.39	21.61
Tamei	17822	47.27	0.52	52.21	94.75	5.25
Nungba	25303	43.97	0.36	55.67	88.26	11.74
Churachandpur	176184	42.51	1.56	53.93	80.07	19.93
Parbung	23995	48.73	0.37	50.90	94.44	5.56

(1)	(2)	(3)	(4)	(5)	(6)	(7)
Thanlon	19209	45.35	0.53	55.12	92.36	7.64
Henglep	20455	47.80	2.02	50.18	93.32	6.68
Samulamlan	13733	41.50	2.50	56.00	75.31	24.69
Churachandpur	80149	37.11	1.55	61.34	63.30	36.70
Singngat	18643	49.75	3.00	47.25	93.19	6.81
Chandel	71014	48.30	4.26	47.44	79.25	20.75
Moreh	20755	44.75	3.61	51.64	78.42	21.58
Machi	10133	52.53	5.04	43.43	93.16	6.84
Chandel	18544	44.78	4.85	50.37	68.08	31.92
Chakpikarong	21582	52.76	3.99	43.25	81.72	18.28
Ukhrul	109275	44.78	1.27	53.95	76.37	23.63
Chingai	18536	43.90	0.75	55.35	87.94	12.06
Ukhrul	61444	42.97	1.25	55.78	69.30	30.70
Kasom Khullen	6341	49.47	0.16	50.37	90.31	9.69
Kamjong	12124	53.18	0.77	46.05	76.72	23.28
Phungyar	10830	44.42	3.48	52.10	86.01	13.99
Jiribam	34046	30.97	5.12	63.91	65.53	34.47
Jiribam	34046	30.97	5.12	63.91	65.53	34.47

Source : Census of India 1991.

3.2.2 Functional Profile of Planning Regions

Of the ten planning regions of the state, four correspond to the valley districts of Imphal East, Imphal West, Thoubal and Bishnupur, five to the hill districts of Senapati, Tamenglong, Churachandpur, Chandel and Ukhrul, and one to the Jiribam area in Barak basin. Table 3.6 presents the functtional characteristics of the planning regions and planning sub-regions, which have been briefly analysed below.

3.2.2.1 Imphal East Planning Region

Imphal East region (Area : 502 km^2/Population 2,96,414), covering the north-eastern part of the Manipur valley, has a participation rate of 32.45 per cent, which is much lower than the state average of 38.56 per cent. The region has the balanced proportion of the agricultural workers and the non-agricultural workers. The large number of non-workers, about 64 per cent of the total population reflects the proportion of massive unemployment prevalent in the region.

Among the planning sub-regions, Sawombung has the largest proportion of main workers and the second lowest of the marginal workers, while Porompat has the largest number of marginal workers as well as of the non-workers. Agricultural workers constitute 64.67 per cent of the labour force in Sawombung, and only 32.08 per cent in Porompat. Non-agricultural workers, representing secondary and tertiary activities, form 67.92 per cent of the main workers in Porompat and only 35.33 per cent in Sawombung.

Imphal East (Porompat), the regional growth centre and growth focus for the entire Manipur, has the lowest proportion of the main workers (22.99 per cent) and the largest of the non-workers (75.72 per cent) in the state. The agricultural workers in this growth centre constitute 5.56 per cent of the main workers and the non-agricultural workers 94.44 per cent, which shows the preponderance of tertiary activities.

3.2.2.2 Imphal West Planning Region

Imphal West region (Area : 555 km²/Population : 3,80,801), comprising the north-western section of the Manipur valley, has a low participation rate of 32.23 per cent. With only two-fifths of its main workers engaged in agriculture, the region records the largest concentration of secondary and tertiary work-force. The region registers the largest proportion of the non-workers, around 65.7 per cent, representing huge unemployment in the core region of the state.

Among its planning sub-regions, Lamphelpat covers the smallest area with the largest concentration of population. It is the most urbanised tract of the state, where less than four per cent of the workforce is employed in agricultural sector and the rest in tertiary and secondary activities. Its other sub-regions resemble their counterparts in rest of the central valley. Among them, Lamsang records a large proportion of main workers (38.56 per cent), with three-fourths of them constituting agricultural workers. Patsoi and Wangoi have almost similar proportion of main workers and non-workers, but the former with larger share of agricultural workers and the later of the non-agricultural workers.

Imphal West (Lamphelpat), the regional growth centre, with preponderence of commercial and administrative functions, has a low proportion of the main workers (27.36 per cent) with only 1.38 per cent of them engaged in agriculture and the rest 98.62 per cent in the secondary and tertiary activities.

3.2.2.3 Thoubal Planning Region

Thoubal region (Area : 514 km²/Poulation : 2,93,958) occupies the south-eastern part of the valley. About 36.63 per cent of its population comprise the main workers and 8.35 per cent the marginal workers. Non-workers, forming 55.02 per cent of population in the region, are the least among the valley regions. Over three-fourths of the workforce in Thoubal region are engaged in agricultural pursuits and only 23.24 per cent in the secondary and tertiary activities. Among the three planning sub-regions, Thoubal has around 53 per cent of the population of non-workers and 37 per cent of the main workers as against over 58 per cent of the non-workers and around 35 per cent of the main workers in Kakching and over 58 per cent of non-workers and 31 per cent of main workers in Lilong. The agricultural workers form around three-fourths of the main workers in all three planning sub-regions of the district, and the non-agricultural workers rest of the work-force.

Thoubal, the regional growth centre, has around one-third of its population (32.92 per cent) classed as main workers, around one-tenth (10.32 per cent) as marginal workers and the rest 56.76 per cent as non-workers. The agricultural workers constitute 64.61 per cent of the main workers in the town showing its rural base irrespective of being the district headquarters.

3.2.2.4 Bishnupur Planning Region

Bishnupur region (Area : 496 km²/Population : 1,80,773) forms the south-western segment of the Manipur valley along the Loktak lake. It has the largest ratio of main workers in the valley (over 38 per cent) with over 55 per cent of the non-workers and six per cent of the marginal workers. About two-thirds of the main workers are engaged in agricultural work and one-third in secondary and tertiary activities. Three planning sub-regions - Bishnupur, Nambol and Moirang testify the regional pattern in their functional characteristics-similar ratio of workers, non-workers, agricultural and non-agricultural workers.

Bishnupur, the regional growth centre, is a small town with historic past, where the main workers form 32.24 per cent of its population, and the non-workers 59.39 per cent. The agricultural and non-agricultural workers are well balanced in the town, 48.34 per cent to 51.66 per cent.

3.2.2.5 Senapati Planning Region

Senapati region (Area : 3271 km²/Population : 2,08,406),

comprising the northern hill tracts peopled by the Naga, Kuki and Nepalese, has the largest proportion of the main workers and the lowest of the non-workers among all the planning regions of the state. Agriculture is the most dominant economic activity employing over nine-tenths of the main workers. Though the region is rich in forest resources, very few people are engaged in forestry. Tertiary activities attract less than one-tenth of the workers. Among the planning sub-regions of Senapati, Mao-Maram has the largest proportion of main workers, about 60.09 per cent, and Saitu the lowest, only 40.79 per cent. Agricultural workers constitute 96.28 per cent of the main workers and the non-agriculturual workers only 3.72 per cent in Purul, while in Saitu agriculture attracts 80.79 per cent of the workers and non-agricultural activities 19.21 per cent.

The regional growth centre-Senapati was a small town prior to 1991 census. It is a developiing central place, where over three-fifths (62.72 per cent) of the population consists of the main workers, and about four-fifths of the workforce is engaged in agriculutral activities.

3.2.2.6 Tamenglong Planning Region

Tamenglong region (Area : 4391 km^2/ population : 86,278), covering the north-western hill section of the state, is inhabited by the Kabui Nagas. The regional population consists of 45.45 per cent main workers, 0.57 per cent marginal workers and 53.98 per cent non-workers. Agriculture employs 88 per cent of the main workers and non-agricultural professions around 12 per cent. In four planning sub-regions the proportion of workers and non-workers is almost similar to the regional pattern but the ratio of agricultural and non-agricultural workers differ to much extent. In Tamei and Tousem only five per cent of the main workers are engaged in tertiary activities as against 21.61 per cent in Tamenglong.

The regional growth centre-Tamenglong is centrally located. It was a town prior to 1991 census. About 36 per cent of its population consists of the main workers and around 57 per cent of them are employed in agriculture and the rest in tertiary activities.

3.2.2.7 Churachandpur Planning Region

Churachandpur region (Area : 4570 km²/Population : 1,76,184), with the largest areal expanse among the planning regions of the state, comprise the south-western hill tracts peopled by the Kuki tribes. The main workers constitute 42.51 per cent of the region's population and the marginal workers only 1.56 per cent. Rest of the population consists of non-workers. About four-fifths of the main workers in the region are engaged in agricultural activities and one-fifth in secondary and tertiary professions. There are six planning sub-regions in the district of which Churachandpur has the largest population (80149) and Samulamlan the smallest (13733). The proportion of main workers ranges from 48.73 per cent in Parbung to 37.11 per cent in Churachandpur. The non-workers constitute only half of the population in Parbung, Henglep and Singngat, and over 55 per cent in other sub-regions. The agricultural workers form 94.44 per cent of the main workers in Parbung and only 63.30 per cent in Churachandpur. The non-agricultural workers form impressive proportions of the workforce in Churachandpur and Samulamlan sub-regions.

Churachandpur, the regional growth centre, is the largest urban settlement of the state after Imphal. Located in the north-eastern corner of the region, the town has only 28 per cent of its people classed as main workers and over 70 per cent non-workers. About two-fifths of its workforce is employed in agriculture and the remaining three-fifths in secondary and tertiary activities.

3.2.2.8 Chandel Planning Region

Chandel region (Area : 3313 km²/Population : 71,014), inhabited mainly by Naga and Kuki tribes, occupies the south-eastern hill tracts of Manipur bordering Myanmar. The main workers form, 48.30 per cent of its population while the ratio of non-workers in its population of 47.44 per cent is the lowest in the entire state. About one-fifth of the main workers are employed in secondary and tertiary activities and four-fifths get sustenance from agriculture. Four planning sub-regions of the district resemble the regional pattern in the proportion of the main workers, marginal workers and non-workers, but differ to much extent in their proportion of agricultural and non-agricultural workers. About two-thirds of the main workers in Chandel are engaged in agricultural activities while their proportion is much higher, over four-fifths, in Moreh and Chakpikarong and over 93 per cent in Machi. Rest of the main workers in the sub-regions are employed in the secondary and tertirary pusuits.

Chandel, the regional growth centre, was a small town prior to 1991 census. Now it is a conglomeration of settlements with urban facilities accommodating district level offices and institutions, where the non-agricultural workers dominate the workforce. The main workers constitute about half of the population of Chandel. Moreh, the only town in the region on the Indo-Myanmar border and a growth point, handles the international trade between our two countries through the land route.

3.2.2.9 Ukhrul Planning Region

Ukhrul region (Area : 4544 km²/Population : 1,09,275), with its rich forest and mineral resources, covers the north-eastern hill section of the state peopled mainly by the Tangkhul Nagas. About 44.78 per cent of its population consists of the main workers, 1.27 per cent marginal workers and 53.95 per cent non-workers. Of the main workers, around three-fourths are engaged in agriculture and one-fourth in the non-agricultural activities. Among the five planning sub-regions of the district, Ukhrul has the lowest proportion of main workers, only 42.97 per cent, and Kamjong the highest, over 53 per cent. Agricultural workers constitute over 90 per cent of the main workers in Kasom Khullen as against 69 per cent in Ukhrul. The ratio of non-agriculutural workers varies from 30.70 per cent in Ukhrul to 9.69 per cent in Kasom Khullen.

The regional growth centre-Ukhrul, a town prior to 1991

census, is centrally located in the district. The main workers form about two-fifths of its population, the marginal workers less than two per cent and the non-workers about 58 per cent. The proportion of the agricultural and non-agricultural workers is well balanced in the labour force of Ukhrul, the largest settlement in the Manipur hills after Churachandpur.

3.2.2.10 Jiribam Planning Region

Jiribam region (Area : 171 km²/Population : 34,046), the smallest of the planning regions both in area and population, lies along the Jiri and Barak rivers in the western part of the state. In its population, the main workers constitute 30.97 per cent, the marginal workers 5.12 per cent and the non-workers 63.91 per cent. Of the main workers, about two-thirds (65.53 per cent) pursue agricultural activities and the rest one-third the non-agricultural professions.

The regional growth centre-Jiribam is a small town in the north-western part of the region. It is the only railhead in Manipur linked with Silchar in the Barak valley of Assam. The main workers form 27.27 per cent of its population, the marginal workers 2.09 per cent and the non-workers 70.64 per cent. About one-fifth of the main wokers, 20.58 per cent, work in agricultural sector while four-fifths, 79.42 per cent, are employed in the secondary and tertiary activities.

3.3 Conclusion

The appraisal of natural and cultural resources of the study region in the preceding chapter and the identification of central places of different orders-growth centres, growth points and service centres and delimitation of their hinterlands in the present highlight the functional and spatial gaps in the socio-economic development of the state. It is, therefore, imperative to bridge these gaps with the help of appropriate strategy incorporating sectoral and spatial development programmes for an overall and integrated development of Manipur. Such a strategy of regional development has been discussed and analysed in the succeeding part of this study.

4

Integrated Regional Development Planning

Regional imbalances exist in the levels of economic development in India, a country with continental dimensions, not only between different states but also within the states between different districts and regions. Such imbalances can be mitigated with the help of necessary resource inputs and implementation of approporiate developmental strategy in the form of specific programmes based on assessment of problems, resources and productive potential in various sectors of economy at different spatial levels.

The importance of a planning strategy for the balanced economic development of various regions in Manipur emanates from a variety of reasons. The strategic location of the state in the extreme north-eastern frontier region of the country, the inequality in the living standards of the hill and valley people, the low per capita income, lack of employment opportunities and inadequate transport facilities all contribute to the need for a programme for the integrated development of the state on a scale and pattern suitable for the purpose.

This chapter reviews the planning efforts of the state initiated since 1951 and their impact on the economic development of various regions and improvements in the living standards of the people, identifies the problems faced in the development of various sectors of economy and charts out developmental strategy with planning proposals formulated and presented in sectoral and spatial frames for the modernization and growth of space economy and balanced regional development of Manipur.

4.1 Review of Five Year Plans

The process of planned economic development was initiated in the country with the launching of the First Five Year Plan in 1951, which aimed at rehabilitation of the economy especially agricultural sector and all-round balanced development ensuring a rising national income and a steady improvement in living standards of the people.

Table 4.1 presents a glimpse of the sectorwise outlay and expenditure incurred during the period of planned development of the state since 1951 in various Five Year Plans and the annual plans.

In Manipur, the First Five Year Plan (1951-56) laid emphasis mainly on the development of transport and communication, which accounted for 72.32 per cent of the plan expenditure of Rs. 102.56 lakhs representing about two-thirds of the total outlay. The social and community services shared 18.59 per cent and the agricultural programmes only 4.25 per cent. The expenditure on irrigation and power development accounted for 4.18 per cent and industry and minerals only 0.66 per cent.

The Second Five Year Plan (1956-61) allocated 37.85 per cent of the total plan expenditure of Rs. 596.93 lakhs to the social and community services sector and 35 per cent for the development of transport and communication. Agriculture and allied services shared 18 per cent of the plan investments, irrigation and power sector about seven per cent, and industry and minerals only two per cent.

The expenditure incurred during the Third Five Year Plan (1961-66) was Rs. 1281.28 lakhs against the outlay of Rs. 1287.56 lakhs. The plan accorded due priority to transport and communication and social and community services sectors spending about 34.25 and 36.26 per cent of investments respectively. The share of expenditure for agriculture and allied services and irrigation and power

Table 4.1
Outlay and Expenditure under Five Year/Annual Plans

(Rs. lakhs)

Head of Department	First Plan (1951-56)		Second Plan (1956-61)		Third Plan (1961-66)		Ad Hoc Plan (1966-69)		Fourth Plan (1969-74)		Fifth Plan (1974-78)	
	Outlay	Expen-diture	Outlay	Expen-diture	Outlay	Expen-diture	Outlay	Expen-diture	Outlay	Expen-diture	Outlay	Expen-diture
Agriculture and allied services	6.70 (4.33)	4.36 (4.25)	121.62 (19.45)	107.59 (18.02)	209.18 (16.25)	184.31 (14.39)	137.94 (13.61)	110.95 (15.41)	407.00 (13.45)	416.00 (13.42)	1259.00 (19.49)	1154.50 (17.33)
Irrigation and power	12.00 (7.75)	4.29 (4.18)	45.00 (7.20)	41.82 (7.01)	119.37 (9.27)	58.56 (4.57)	115.00 (11.35)	89.19 (12.39)	424.88 (14.05)	384.00 (12.39)	1947.00 (30.14)	2056.78 (30.87)
Industry and minerals	0.60 (0.39)	0.68 (0.66)	13.06 (2.09)	12.08 (2.02)	49.39 (3.84)	35.28 (2.75)	44.00 (4.34)	18.90 (2.63)	117.22 (3.88)	215.00 (6.93)	489.00 (7.57)	474.76 (7.13)
Transport and communication	91.89 (59.32)	74.17 (72.32)	215.46 (34.47)	208.90 (35.00)	441.00 (34.25)	503.23 (39.27)	428.60 (42.28)	316.86 (44.02)	1170.85 (38.71)	1260.00 (40.65)	1305.00 (20.20)	1480.60 (22.23)
Social and community services	43.70 (28.21)	19.06 (18.59)	229.35 (36.69)	225.93 (37.85)	466.87 (36.26)	491.87 (38.39)	260.20 (25.67)	152.07 (21.12)	897.05 (29.65)	813.51 (26.24)	1175.00 (18.19)	1230.92 (18.48)
Economic general services	- -	- -	0.62 (0.10)	0.61 (0.10)	1.75 (0.13)	8.03 (0.63)	27.84 (2.75)	31.92 (4.43)	8.00 (0.26)	11.49 (0.37)	285.00 (4.41)	254.35 (3.96)
Total	154.89 (100.00)	102.56 (100.00)	625.11 (100.00)	596.93 (100.00)	1287.56 (100.00)	1281.28 (100.00)	1013.58 (100.00)	719.89 (100.00)	3025.00 (100.00)	3100.00 (100.00)	6460.00 (100.00)	6661.91 (100.00)

Agriculture and allied services sector also includes cooperation and rural development.
Irrigation and power sector includes energy too.
Economic and general services also include science and technology.

Table 4.1 (*Contd.*)

(Rs. lakhs)

Head of Development	Ad hoc Rolling Plan (1978-80)		Sixth Plan (1980-85)		Seventh Plan (1985-90)		Annual Plan (1990-92)		Eighth Plan (1992-97)		Ninth Plan (1997-2002)
	Outlay	Expenditure	Outlay	Expenditure	Outlay	Expenditure	Outlay	Expenditure	Outlay	Expenditure	Outlay
Agriculture and allied services	1080.00 (18.20)	1235.77 (19.56)	4539.00 (18.40)	4742.83 (19.51)	7095.00 (16.50)	7932.62 (15.71)	4906.00 (13.59)	4753.79 (13.61)	10679.00 (10.91)	11831.83 (10.12)	24437.00 (10.07)
Irrigation and power	1740.00 (29.31)	1868.50 (29.57)	6356.00 (25.77)	6210.12 (25.54)	11442.00 (26.61)	14132.35 (27.99)	14277.53 (39.54)	13530.45 (38.74)	36365.00 (37.14)	39182.81 (33.50)	65594.00 (27.03)
Industry and minerals	364.00 (6.13)	318.17 (5.03)	1498.00 (6.07)	1352.44 (5.56)	2430.00 (5.65)	2759.61 (5.47)	1713.24 (4.74)	1617.62 (4.63)	3980.00 (4.07)	4508.17 (3.85)	12651.00 (5.21)
Transport and communication	1171.00 (19.73)	1253.72 (19.84)	3517.00 (14.26)	3706.51 (15.25)	7150.00 (16.63)	7466.83 (14.79)	4928.59 (13.65)	5023.08 (14.38)	16060.00 (16.40)	19943.11 (17.05)	39968.00 (16.47)
Social and community services	1334.00 (22.47)	1470.24 (23.26)	7973.00 (32.33)	7410.26 (30.48)	12687.00 (29.50)	15019.55 (29.75)	8597.17 (23.81)	8321.92 (23.83)	26040.00 (26.60)	35665.16 (30.49)	61964.00 (25.54)
Economic and general services	247.00 (4.16)	173.16 (2.74)	782.00 (3.17)	890.16 (3.66)	2196.00 (5.11)	3175.23 (6.29)	1687.00 (4.67)	1679.49 (4.81)	4776.00 (4.88)	5840.27 (4.99)	38055.00 (15.68)
Total	5936.00 (100.00)	6319.56 (100.00)	24665.00 (100.00)	24312.32 (100.00)	43000.00 (100.00)	50486.19 (100.00)	36109.53 (100.00)	34926.35 (100.00)	97900.00 (100.00)	116971.35 (100.00)	242669.00 (100.00)

Figures in brackets indicate percentage

Source : Planning Department, Government of Manipur.

declined, and for industry and minerals and economic and general services improved slightly.

During the ad hoc plans, spread over 1966-69, the pattern of investment remained almost similar to that of the Third Plan. The transport and communication sector accounted for 44 per cent of total expenditure followed by social services sector (21.12 per cent), agriculture and allied services (15.41 per cent) and irrigation and power (12.39 per cent). The share of industry and minerals declined slightly and of economic and general services improved immensely during the ad hoc plan period.

The total expenditure during the Fourth Five Year Plan (1969-74) was Rs. 31 crores, a little more than the plan outlay of Rs. 30.25 crores, of which 40.65 per cent was spent on the improvement of transport and communication and 26.24 per cent on social and community services. Agricultural programmes, and irrigation and power sectors accounted for 13.42 per cent and 12.39 per cent of the plan expenditure respectively. Industry and minerals sector got adequate attention during this plan. It accounted for 6.93 per cent of the total investment as against 2.63 per cent during the Third Plan.

The Fifth Five Year Plan (1974-78) could not complete its full period and was abandoned a year earlier due to change in the government in the centre. During this plan, the special attention was given to the development of irrigation and power, which accounted for 30.87 per cent of the total expenditure of Rs. 66.62 crores. More than two-fifths of the plan resources were mobilized for improvement of transport and communication, and social and community services. With 17.33 per cent of the investment on agricultural development and 7.13 per cent on industry and minerals, the Fifth Plan laid a sound base for economic development of the state. The economic and general services attracted less than four per cent of the plan investment.

The Fifth Plan was followed by ad hoc rolling annual plans

during 1978-80 in which Rs. 63.20 crores were spent as against the outlay of Rs. 59.36 crores. In these annual plans maximum stress was laid on the development of irrigation and power (29.57 per cent) followed by social and community services (23.26 per cent), transport and communcation (19.84 per cent) and agricultural programmes (19.56 per cent). The share of industry and minerals, and economic and general services, however, declined during this period.

During the Sixth Five Year Plan (1980-85), out of the total expenditure of Rs. 243.12 crores, 30.48 per cent was spent on social and community services, 25.54 per cent on irrigation and power, 19.51 per cent on agricultural programmes and 15.25 per cent on improvement of transport and communication. The investments on industry and minerals, and general and economic services remained at a lower pace than the Fifth Plan.

The Seventh Five Year Plan (1985-90) expenditure of Rs. 504.86 crores was much larger than the outlay of Rs. 430 crores. Maximum stress was given to the improvement of social and community services (29.75 per cent) during the plan followed by irrigation and power development (27.99 per cent), and improvements of agricultural and allied services (15.71 per cent) and transport and communication (14.79 per cent). Industry and minerals, and economic and general services each attracted a little over five per cent of the plan investments.

Two annual plans, 1990-91 and 1991-92, which preceded the Eighth Plan had a combined outlay of Rs. 361.1 crores of which only Rs. 349.26 crores could be spent. During these two years maximum emphasis was given to the development of irrigation and power which accounted for about two-thirds (38.74 per cent) of the investments followed by social and community services sharing about one-fourth (23.83 per cent) of it. For the improvements in the transport and communication sector and agriculture and allied services investments to the tune of 14.38 per cent and 13.61 per cent were made during the period. The proportion of expenditure on industry and minerals, and economic and general services was less than five per cent in each sector as against over five per cent during the Seventh Plan.

The Eighth Five Year Plan (1992-97) incurred an expenditure of Rs. 1169.71 crores as against the outlay of Rs. 979.00 crores. It laid maximum emphasis on the irrigation and power development (33.50 per cent) followed by improvement of social and community services (30.49 per cent), transport and communication (17.05 per cent), and development of agriculture and allied services (10.12 per cent). The economic and general services utilised 4.99 per cent of the Eighth Plan expenses and the industry and minerals sector only 3.85 per cent.

The Ninth Five Year Plan (1997-2002) was launched in April, 1997 with an impressive outlay of Rs. 2426.69 crores, with major emphasis on the development of infrastructure-irrigation and power, transport and communication and social and community services. The irrigation and power sector has been allocated 27.03 per cent of the plan outlay, social and community services 25.54 per cent and transport and communication 16.47 per cent. Agriculture and allied services including rural development have been provided 10.07 per cent of the plan resources while the share of economic and general services including science and technology will be 15.68 per cent and those of industry and minerals sector 5.21 per cent.

An analysis of the pattern of outlay and expenditure on different sectors of development since the First Five Year Plan, reveals the decline in the emphasis on the development of agriculture and allied services and transport and communication sectors and an enhanced stress on the improvement of irrigation and power and social and community services over the years in the development planning of the state. The industry and minerals and economic and general services had almost a constant ratio of investment during the plans in the range of four to five per cent, except for the later in the current Ninth Plan outlay.

Planning as an instrument of programming economic development has not affected various sectors of economy and sections of people living in different parts of the state in the same proportion. As such, sectoral and regional imbalances exist in the valley and hill areas of Manipur with vast differences in the living standards of the people inhabiting these ecological zones. Accordingly, the sectoral and regional issues in the planning process have been appraised, analysed and presented in the following sections.

4.2 Sectoral Planning

Different sectors of economy in the state have their own sets of problems and prospects for mitigating them. Planning proposals for these sectors have been discussed herewith based on their feasibility for regional development planning. The sectoral issues in the planning process have been divided into the following :

a. Agriculture and allied services sector
b. Irrigation and power sector
c. Industry and minerals sector
d. Transport and communication sector
e. Social and community services sector
f. Economic and general services sector

It is assumed that almost all problems of the state find place within these dimensions. Accordingly the planning proposals for these sectors of economy have been discussed and presented in this section.

4.2.1 Agriculture and Allied Services

This sector of planning includes crop husbandry, soil and water conservation, animal husbandry, dairy development, fisheries, forestry and wildlife, plantations and rural development.

Agriculture, being the mainstay of the population, assumes pivotal role in the regional development. The problem of agricultural development in the state is the problem of introducing improved cropping patterns, improved techniques, and maximising inputs of resources in agriculture. Uneconomic holdings, with higher man-land ratio and lower carrying capacity of land, low level of agricultural infrastructure and agricultural extension services affect the development of agriculture in the state.

Manipur, which was once a surplus state, is not self-sufficient in food grains production. Rice, being the main food crop both for the valley and hills, has witnessed a decline in its production trend during the last decade mainly due to natural calamities like droughts and floods besides everincreasing population. The situation on the food front had been grim in the absence of supportive measures like diversification of crops, irrigation facilities, lack of infrastructure etc. As such, the state has to import about one-third of its food requirements from the central pool.

Jhuming is widely practised in the hill areas, where with increasing pressure on land, jhum cycle is shrinking continuously creating ecological problems like soil erosion, deforestation, landslides, siltation of river beds, etc. Soil conservation in the hills and water conservation in the valley have, therefore, to be taken up to maintain ecological balance and agricultural productivity level in the state.

Horticultural production of fruits and vegetables is not sufficient to meet the local demand resulting in their large scale imports. The ecological conditions are well suited for producing fruits in the hills and vegetables in the valley. Attempts have to be made to extend area under these crops.

The quality of livestock and poultry is poor and the quantity of fish production inadequate irrespective of sound environmental conditions suited to the enhancement of their quality and quantity.

Forests, covering about four-fifths of the state area, contribute too little to the state's net domestic product-mainly due to poor management practices including indiscriminate exploitation, jhuming, forest fires etc. Wild life in the forests in the hill areas and lake environs in the valley can be exploited for promotion of tourism.

Cooperation can be of immense help in the development of agriculture, allied and non-farm sectors and in association with gram panchayats and village councils, can bring faster pace of rural development throughout the state.

Agriculture and allied sector, therefore, needs to be augmented and developed for providing basic necessities to the people-food, clothing and employment. Accordingly following planning measures are proposed to transform this sector :

a. Adjustments in agricultural landuses and land development programmes : Over nine-tenths of the cropped land, due to monocultivation of rice, remains vacant for five to seven months. Rabi crops and vegetables can be grown over them during this period. In the hill areas, to minimise the intensity of jhuming, land development programmes can be taken up by terracing the favourable slopes for agricultural purposes and use of jhum lands for horticultural uses and dairy farming.

b. Reorientation in cropping patterns and development of irrigation : With development of irrigation facilities double and multiple cropping patterns may emerge on the agricultural landscape of the central valley and Barak basin. Tea and rubber plantations, which are currently confined to Jiribam area in Barak basin, may be extended to Tamenglong and Tipaimukh areas in Manipur western hills having similar ecological conditions. Cotton cultivation on the slopes overlooking the valley, sugarcane and wheat in the northern part of the valley and maize throughout the hills alongwith fruits, vegetables and spices like chillies and ginger can be taken up to augment income of the farmers and availability of raw materials for the industries.

c. Adoption of soil conservation and flood control measures : Soil erosion in the hill areas and siltation of the lake and river beds in the valley result in widespread floods damaging the crops, houses and domestic animals. As such, there is need for effective soil conservation and flood control measures to check these calamities. Massive afforestation in the hills and social and farm forestry in the valley have to be taken up to conserve the soils, curb the floods and check the landslides and siltation.

d. Creation of agricultural complexes : As the size of land holdings is shrinking and gradually becoming uneconomic for agricultural operation, large agricultural complexes should be planned by integrating all marginal and small holdings together at the level of cluster of villages, where cooperative farming measures may be adopted for higher returns. About 10 to 20 such complexes may be planned in each planning sub-region.Consolidation of land holdings and reorganisation of farming have to precede the creation of such complexes.

e. Establishment of extension centres : For rapid transformation and development of agriculture, existing extension centres at the block and district levels should be strengthened to educate the farmers in modern agricultural technology. The village level workers at the service centres should provide such services to the farmers in the villages.

f. Afforestation : The jhuming practices should be restricted to the lower slopes. The critical slopes, i.e. above 45^0, have to be kept under dense forest cover. The abandoned jhum lands should be brought under mixed cultivation of grass species and trees of economic importance. Beyond this zone timber plants like teak, pine, and oak may be planted to make the forests economically rich and superb. On the land adjacent to settlements and on the foothills, cultivation of commercial fruits like mango, banana, orange, pineapple and citrus fruits etc. may be taken up on impressive scale to enhance the income of the people dependent on this sector.

g. Development of fisheries : With abundance of water bodies-lakes and rivers, the central valley and the Barak basin have ample scope of developing fisheries. Ths fishing methods and practices in the state are traditional with low per capita daily output. It is, therefore, proposed to develop fishing on commercial lines by introduction of new techniques, improved seeds, better storage, packing and processing facilities around Loktak lake. Four fish processing plants, one each at Thanga, Moirang, Ningthoukhong and Mayang Imphal, are proposed for augmenting the fishing industry.

h. Dairy development : With large number of livestock and huge domestic market, the state is well suited to develop dairying. At present there is a milk processing plant at Porompat. It is recommended to establish similar plants at Kangpokpi and Saikul where large number of Nepalese are engaged in animal husbandry and dairying activities.

i. Community development : Gram panchayats and village councils with enhanced budget and executive powers can provide institutional frame for rural and community development. It is, therefore, recommended to involve these grassroot institutions in the rural and community development activities particularly in implementation of integrated rural development programme (IRDP) and Jawahar Rozgar Yojana (JRY) for the upliftment of the rural poor.

j. Development of cooperatives : Cooperatives can bring faster development in agriculture and allied services. As such, it is proposed to orgainse cooperatives at the service centre level, and in all the villages with above 1000 population, to provide credit, marketing and infrastructures-inputs, machineries, implements etc. for augmenting the agricultural production. The Gram Panchayat Level Multi-Purpose Cooperative Societies (GPLMPCS) in the valley and Large-size Agricultural Multi-Purpose Societies (LAMPS) in the hills provide agricultural credit, chemical fertilizers, farm machines through hiring centres and run consumers' stores. Cooperative societies can also bring development in the allied sectors like fisheries, dairying, plantations and forestry.

k. Effective rural linkage : To bring dynamism to the growth of agricultural and allied sector effective linkage and assured connectivity is a precondition. It is, therefore, proposed to link all the settlements by metalled roads in the valley and by at least unmetalled roads in the hills.

4.2.2 Irrigation and Power

This sector of planning includes major, medium and minor irrigation, flood control and power.

Manipur, being an agricultural state, needs irrigation facilities for utmost development of its agricultural sector. Of the seven major and medium irrigation projects taken up so far, Singda, Thoubal and Khuga are multi-purpose projects, Loktak Lift Irrigation a major project, and Khoupum dam, Imphal barrage and Sekmai barrage are medium projects, which will have an ultimate irrigation potential of 1022.4 km^2, of which 580 km^2 have been created so far. At present, about four-fifths of the irrigation potential is being utilised. Minor irrigation projects, particularly in the hill areas, have an estimated irrigation potential of 1670 km^2, of which only 270 km^2 has been created till now, with two-thirds of it being utilised for irrigating agricultural fields.

Of late, floods have become a regular feature in the central valley causing heavy damages to standing crops, properties, loss of human lives and livestock. Floods are the resultant feature of heavy deforestation and excessive jhuming in the upper catchment areas of rivers flowing in the basin, reclamation of lowlying areas which earlier served as flood control measures-construction and maintenance of river embankments and improvement of drainage channels have been taken up to check the floods in Merakhong, Nambul and Wangjing river basins and Lamphelpat area of Imphal.

The state is endowed with a rich hydro-power potential. With the commissioning of the Loktak Hydro-Electric Project in 1983, the power position in the state has improved considerably. A number of mini hydel plants and diesel generating sets have been installed to electrify the administrative headquarters in the hill areas. But the power distribution system is not able to cope up with the requirements of the domestic consumption, street lighting and industry. About 90 per cent of the villages are electrified but power supply in most of them is minimal. Non-conventional sources of energy-biogas, solar and wind energy are being explored to satisfy the power requirements in parts of the state.

Irrigation and power sector, being basic to the agricultural and industrial development and for improvement in the living standards of the people, has to be developed and augmented to meet the growing needs of the society. Following measures are, therefore, recommended to augment the irrigation and power potential in Manipur :

a. Construction of dams and barrages : The swift flowing streams and rivers should be harnessed by constructing dams in steps to store enough water to fulfil the water requirements of the neighbourhood for drinking and irrigation. Larger barrages across the rivers can be utilised for generating power in mini hydel plants to meet the local requirements.

b. Afforestation in upper reaches of the rivers : Programme for growing dense forests in the upper reaches will check not only the massive soil erosion but will also stop the siltation of river and lake beds, which enhances the spread of flood water in wider areas.

c. Effective diversion of river courses : Nambul river, which passes through densely settled areas of Imphal city, can be diverted to the south prior to reaching the city to check the fury of flood experienced too often in Imphal area.

d. Strengthening the river embankments : All the major rivers of the state have shallow channels, which get inundated during the rains causing flood in the neighbourhood. The river embankments have to be strengthened and their channels excavated to keep rain water in manageable limits.

e. Generation/purchase of power : The state's share in the Loktak power is not sufficient for its needs. As such, either new power houses are commissioned or efforts made to purchase more power from the Loktak project by enhancing the state's share. The proposed Tipaimukh and Loktak downstream projects will provide ample energy to meet the growing demands besides bringing enough revenue to the state to augment its financial resources.

4.2.3 Industry and Minerals

This sector of planning includes industries, sericulture and mining.

Manipur is one of the industrially backward states of the country mainly for its chronic infrastructural constraints. Manfacturing contributes a meagre 3.21 per cent to the State Domestic Product and employs only 8.11 per cent of the workforce as per 1991 Census. Prior to the Fourth Five Year Plan the industries in the state consisted of only handloom weaving and handicrafts. Now the state has a khandsari sugar factory, a spinning mill, a cement plant, a vanaspati factory, a bamboo chipping plant, an electronics unit, a cycle assembly plant and a drug formulation unit.

Industries in the state suffer from inadequate and untimely supply of raw materials, low wages in the unorganised sector, low productivity in the cottage industries and lack of marketing infrastructure.

Sericulture development has been quite impressive since the Fourth Plan. Oak tasar, mulberry and sericulture have been developed with establishment of over 127 sericulture centres in different parts of the state. A reeling and spinning factory has also been established to process the silk produced in the sericulture centres.

Systematic geological mapping and survey of selected areas having mineral potential mainly in the ultrabasic belt in Chandel and Ukhrul districts have been taken up in the mining sector.

For economic diversification and solving the massive unemployment, the rapid industrialisation has to be taken up on priority basis. Following programmes are recommended for the growth and development of industries and mining sector in the state :

a. Creation of raw materials depots and complexes : The significant problem faced in industrial development relates to untimely and inadequate supply of raw materials to the industrial units. It is, therefore, proposed to establish raw materials depots in each service centre and raw material complexes at each growth point to ensure easy availability of raw materials to the workers in the cottage industries.

b. State purchase of industrial products : To save the producers from the contractors and middlemen state purchase of industrial products is proposed. The raw material depots and complexes may be entrusted with this task. Otherwise, industrial cooperatives may be established to provide marketing network for handloom and handicraft products.

c. Industrial training facilities : To train the industrial workers in adopting new techniques, training centres should be established at the growth points and growth centres. Such centres may also review the production of industrial units to bring accountability on the part of the producer.

d. Establishment of new industrial units : To solve the problem of increasing unemployment a large number of small industries are proposed to be established. Such industries should comprise units manufacturing value added articles involoving low weight and volume and having large domestic market. Forest and mineral based industries like furniture, sports goods, cement, bricks and building materials can be established in the hill areas and agro-based industries in the central valley and the Barak basin to solve the problem of unemployment and utilisation of resource potential of the state.

4.2.4 Transport and Communication

Transport and communication system constitutes the most important infrastructure for the development of production and distribution system. In absence of rail and water transport, roads are the main arteries and veins through which the stream of economic development activities flow. Road communication affects almost all sectors of economy, such as irrigation, power, water supply, agriculture and industries, etc. However, at present, many sub-divisional and block headquarters and administrative centres particularly in the hill areas of the state are not provided with good linkage. Besides a large number of villages, including proposed service centres, are not connected by roads.

The existing road system suffer from various deficiencies like inadequate crust thickness, narrow and weak bridges, insufficient cross drainage works. etc. Transport and communication sector, therefore, has to be strengthened and improved for speedier socio-economic transformation of the state. Following proposals are made for the development of this sector :

a. Linkage to all the settlements : All the villages in the central valley and Barak basin should be provided effective linkage by improvement of the existing roads and laying out of new roads. Similarly, in the hills where villages are too many and too small, it is recommended that all the villages over 500 population be linked with roads. The transport network will lead to the proper utilisation of the natural resources and socio-economic transformation of the state.

b. Water transport in the Loktak region : The villages along the lake margin and island settlements should be provided mechanized water transport for better prices for fish and other products. Rivers Jiri and Barak in the Barak basin area can be utilised for water transport to connect most of the villages in the Jiribam sector.

c. Extension of rail link : The rail link connecting Jiribam with Silchar may be extended eastward atleast upto Maku to facilitate economic exploitation of the Barak drainage bamboo forests. The project to link Karong in Senapati district with Diphu in Assam by a broad gauge railway has been initiated by the Central Government. In the next stage, these rail links may be extended further upto Imphal.

d. Air linkage : At present Imphal is connected by air with Delhi, Calcutta, Silchar and Guwahati but the frequency of the services is not adequate. It is, therefore, proposed to link Imphal with Delhi and Calcutta by daily services of the Indian Airlines or some commercial airways to facilitate movement of the people, mail and goods effectively with speed.

e. Development or urban transport : The road system in and around Imphal is under acute traffic pressure. Special attention has, therefore, to be given to improve and augment transport facilities in the Greater Imphal area.

4.2.5 Social and Community Services

This sector of planning envisages to improve the quality of life of the people and covers programmes on education, including adult and technical education, sports and youth affairs, art and culture, medical and health services, water supply and sanitation, housing and urban development, information and publicity, social welfare, labour and employment, and nutrition.

Manipur is not far behind other states in liberal education, and technical and professional education. The state has a polytechnic and an engineering college besides some reserved seats in the engineering colleges in other states. The hill areas suffer from lack of institutions of higher learning. The female literacy is lower almost throughout the state for want of girls' schools. In the remote hill areas there are many schoolless villages.

Similar situation persists in the field of medical and health services. The availability of doctors and nurses and beds in the hill districts is meagre while it is abundant in the valley districts. Most of the health centres, sub-centres and dispensaries in the rural, tribal and hill areas are casually visited by the medical staff making such institutions ineffective for the people.

Sports facilities and youth activities have not made much impact in the rural tracts of the state both in the valley and the hills. Development of art and culture too have been confined to the urban tracts, particularly the district headquarters, Other activities in this sector like water supply and sanitation, housing and urban development, labour and employment have been developed mostly to satisfy the needs and requirements of the urban people. However, the welfare programmes for the weaker sections of the society including women and children, scheduled castes and scheduled tribes have made their headway even to the rural areas throughout the state.

Social and community services sector, aiming at the qualitative improvement of human resources and manpower in the context of overall development, is pivotal to the planning in all sectors of economy. Accordingly the following proposals have been made to promote this important sector of planning :

a. Education for all : Education, being the most important input for development, has to be imparted to all to make the socio-economic planning realistic and mass-based. Mass education can be achieved only through the participation of educated persons in this mission. The role of formal, informal and adult education should be identified and entrusted to educate the entire population. All the school-less villages should be provided at least primary schools. In the hill areas, where villages in some parts are too small, educational facilities may be provided by grouping them in clusters. All the service centres in the hills may be provided with high schools and in the valley with the facilities upto higher secondary education.

b. Institutions of higher education : At present, only one district headquarters-Senapati, and one autonomous district headquarters-Kangpokpi lack facilities for college education. It is, therefore, proposed to establish colleges in these two places. The existing colleges at Tamenglong, Chandel and Jiribam have to be strengthened to make them appropriate centres of higher education. The growth points-block and subdivisional headquarters should have facilities upto higher secondary/junior college level. As such, higher secondary schools or junior colleges are proposed for all the growth points where they do not exist. Colleges are also proposed to be established in the urban centres in the valley where facilties for higher education are not available.

c. Technical education centres : Functional education is of utmost importance in human resource development. There are six industrial training institutes, located at Imphal, Ukhrul, Churachandpur, Senapati, Tamenglong and Jiribam and a polytechnic and engineering college at Imphal imparting technical education. For larger coverage and dissemination of technical knowhow, it is recommended to establish industrial training institutes at Thoubal, Bishnupur and Chandel and a polytechnic at Churachandpur besides the girls' polytechnic at Imphal.

d. Medical and health facilities : In qualitative improvement of human resources health care facilities are of vital importance. The state does not lack in number of health care units-primary heatlh centres (PHC) and sub-centres (PHSC), community health centres (CHC), hospitals and dispensaries, but suffers most for the lack of inputs-medical and health services personnel, medicines and equipments in those units. It is, therefore, proposed to strengthen the existing health care units by equipping them with adequate staff, equipments and medicines. It is further recommended that the PHCs at the growth points be upgraded into CHCs and PHSCs at service centres into PHCs. In all the villages above 500 population in the hills and 1000 population in the valley, there should be mini-health units/dispensaries manned by subordinate medical staff to look after the medical and health problems of the people in the rural areas. For the villages with less than 500 population medical and health care facilities may be provided through the mobile dispensaries.

e. Sports and youth affairs : To harness youth power for balanced development adequate sports facilities have to be provided in each and every locality. Sports clubs, youth clubs and centres with proper infrastructural support may prove immensely helpful in executing anti-drugs, social service and afforestation programmes in the rural areas. It is accordingly proposed to open youth centres in all the villages above one thousand population and sports clubs in all the villages above 500 population. Educated youths should also be involved in programmes like eradication of illiteracy and poverty from the rural areas. The Khuman Lampak Sports Complex constructed for the National Games 1999 is one of the best sports complexes in the country with a number of stadia, swimming pool, velodrome and shooting range.

f. Urban development and water supply : The fast pace of urban growth and the rapid increase in the urban population necessitate programmes for balanced development of the urban areas in the state. With growing population, the urban centres are fast turning into slums. Corrective measures have, therefore, to be adopted in this regard. Water supply in almost all the towns is inadequate. It is to be augmented to meet the needs of the people. Similarly, most of the towns suffer from poor transport system which has to be improved to bear the everincreasing traffic pressure over them. The growth centres and growth points should be recognised as urban centres and developed accordingly to meet the requirements of their hinterlands.

g. Popularisation of art and culture : Manipur is famous for its art and culture. By popularising the classical Manipuri Ras and folk dances, artistic handicrafts, scenic spots, unique flora and fauna, the state can find a place of pride on the tourist map of the country. As such, is is proposed to develop scenic spots of the state with year round dance and cultural festivals to attract the tourists, both internal and external, to make tourism an important sector of income generation.

h. Extension of social/tribal welfare programmes : Social and tribal welfare programmes implemented till now aiming at the improvement of weaker sections of the society have to be strengthened to bring these unpriviledged people to the level of general population. Special training programmes may be taken up to train the women, tribal and backward people enabling them to take up vocations like weaving, tailoring, manufacture of domestic consumables like candles, match boxes, furniture, stone articles, small implements, etc. with financial support from the government and financial institutions. In the hill areas schemes like dairying, poultry, mushroom production, coffee, rubber and cardamom plantations, etc. can be implemented to raise the income level of the people improving the quality of their life.

Fig. 4.1 shows the location of existing and proposed administrative, educational, health and infrastructural facilities/services in the state.

4.2.6 Economic and General Services

This sector of planning includes science, technology and environment, planning, tourism, district councils, and public works. The plan outlay for this sector was a meagre sum of Rs. 62,000 during the Second Plan, which stands at Rs. 380.55 crores in the current Ninth Plan.

A number of programmes have been initiated under this sector to popularise science and technology, environmental awareness, execution of scientific researches, effective planning measures, administration of hill districts and public works.

As this sector plays an important role in integrated regional development of the state, following measures are proposed to enhance its effectiveness :

a. Scientific researches and technological innovations should be taken up for exploitation and utilisation of natural resources-vast forest wealth, water resources, fertile land in the valley and Barak basin, and of course rich human resources.

b. Environmental awareness for maintenance of fragile ecological

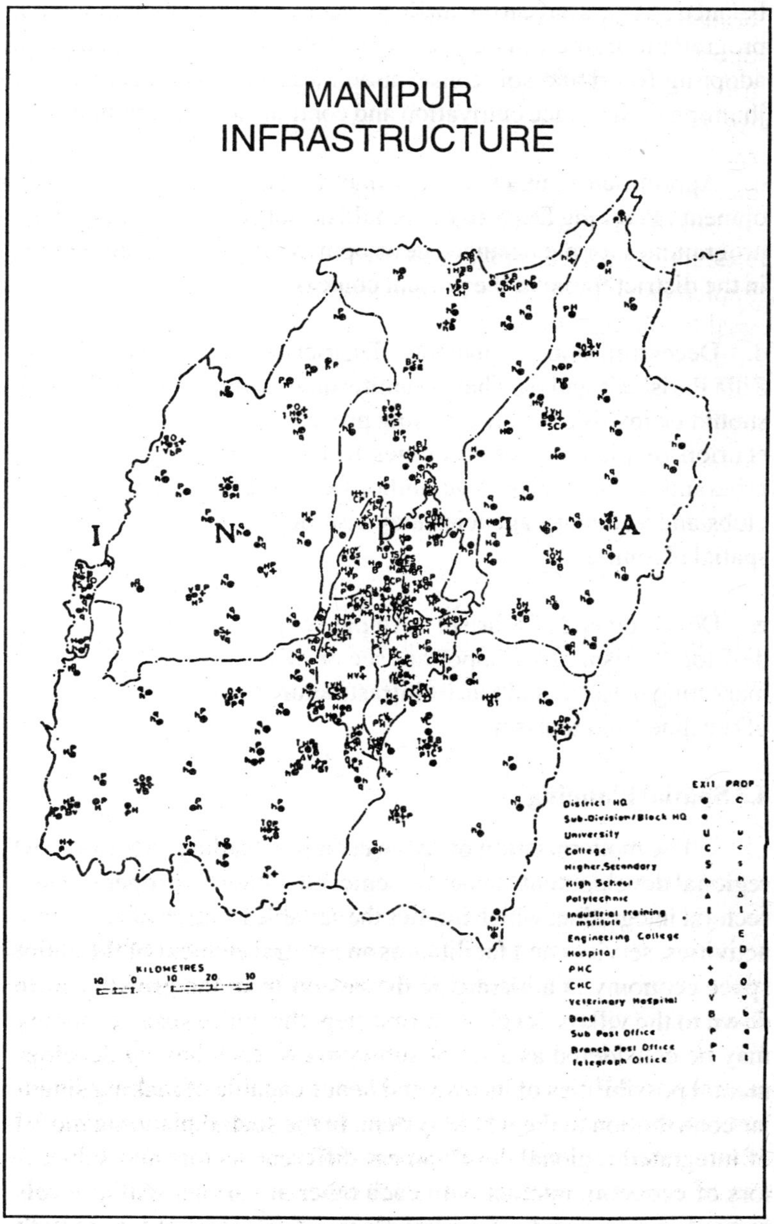
MANIPUR
INFRASTRUCTURE
I N D I A
KILOMETRES
10 0 10 20 30
EXIT PROP
District HQ
Sub-Division/Block HQ
University
College
Higher Secondary
High School
Polytechnic
Industrial Training Institute
Engineering College
Hospital
PHC
CHC
Veterinary Hospital
Bank
Sub Post Office
Branch Post Office
Telegraph Office

Fig. 4.1

balance : Efforts have to be made to make environmental protection programme in the hills a success to enthuse the tribal people in adopting forest and soil consevation measures by replacement of jhuming with terrace cultivation and contour farming methods.

c. Appropriate planning programmes for balanced regional development : Planning Department should initiate perspective planning programmes for the balanced development of various spatial units, in the district frame in the present context.

d. Decentralisation of planning : District Councils in the hills, and Zilla Parishads and panchayat samitis in the valley and Barak basin should be involved in the planning process for formulation and execution of planning programmes to make planning a people's programme. Help of village authorities, gram panchayats, youth clubs and voluntary agencies may also be taken up in this task of spatial planning.

e. Development of toùrism : Ample scope exists in the state to develop tourism as an important sector of economy. With proper marketing network and tourist infrastructure the state can earn a lot of revenue from tourism.

4.3 Spatial Planning

The modernisation of space economy leading to the desired regional development cannot be achieved without a proper spatial-sectoral integration, which implies the suitable location of economic activities, services and facilities as an integral element of the entire space economy in a hierarchic dimension from the growth centre down to the village level. As a first step, the entire space economy may be considered as a set of sub-systems, each having developmental possibilities of its own and hence capable of making singular contribution to the whole system. In the spatial planning model of integrated regional development different sectors and sub-sectors of economy interact with each other at various spatial levels formed of hinterlands of central places of different orders-growth centres, growth points and service centres, which differ to much extent in levels of development analysed with help of poverty situation and selected economic indicators.

4.3.1 Levels of Development

The planned economic development of the state has brought wide disparities in the socio-economic situation in various districts reflected in variations in the magnitude of poverty presented in Table 4.2 and portrayed in Fig. 4.2

Table 4.2
Magnitude of Poverty in Manipur

District	% of population below poverty line
Imphal East/West	48.87
Thoubal	42.02
Bishnupur	38.01
Senapati	21.57
Tamenglong	55.10
Churachandpur	51.78
Chandel	64.07
Ukhrul	52.28
Manipur	45.06

Source : Eighth Five Year Plan 1992-97.

The hill districts, except Senapati, are reeling under acute poverty mainly for underutilisation of their natural resources due to lack of infrastructure. In Chandel district, over 64 per cent of the people live below the poverty line and in Churachandpur, Ukhrul and Tamenglong between 51 and 55 per cent. In Senapati, the poverty infested people form 21.57 per cent of population, the lowest magnitude in the entire state, for better connectivity and enterprising nature of the people. In the valley, the proportion of population living below the poverty line ranges between 38.01 per cent in Bishnupur to 48.87 per cent in Imphal East and West as against

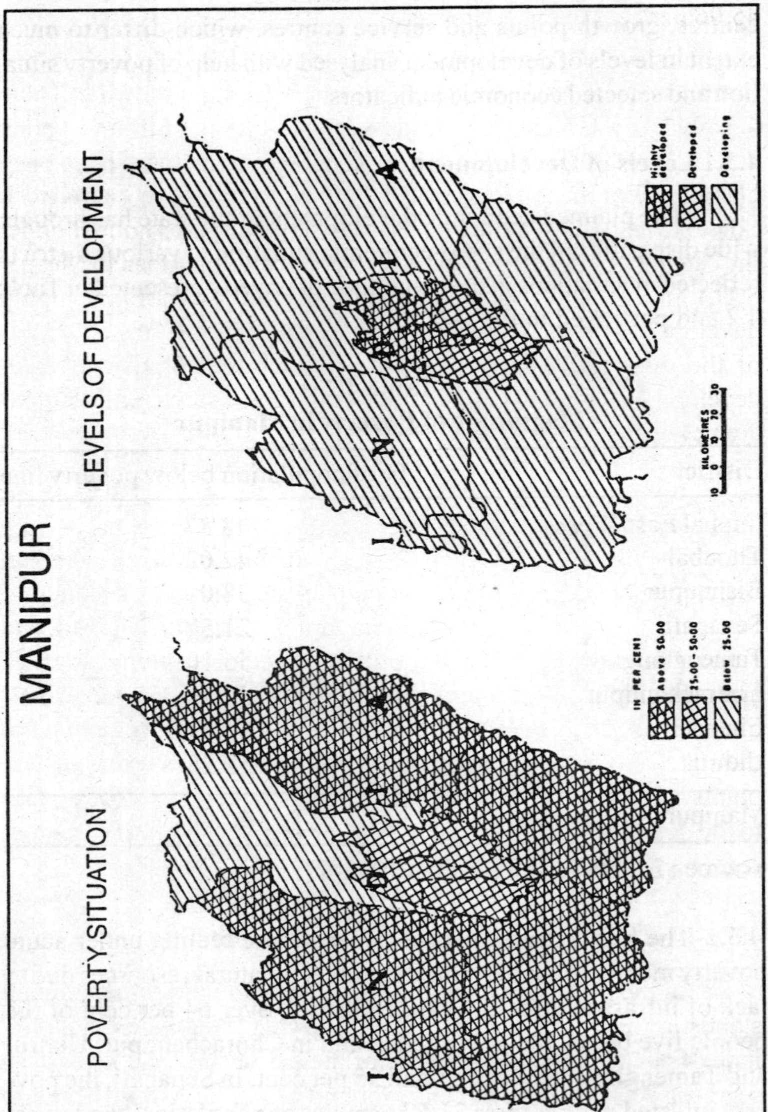
MANIPUR
POVERTY SITUATION
LEVELS OF DEVELOPMENT
IN PER CENT
Above 50.00
25.00 - 50.00
Below 25.00
Highly developed
Developed
Developing
KILOMETRES
10 0 10 20 30
I N D I A

Fig. 4.2

45.06 per cent in the entire state.

An analysis of selected economic indicators shown in Table 4.3 reveals the disparities in development of the hill and valley districts. All the five hill districts as per weighted score have been classed under the category of developing districts (score between S.D. to Mean), two valley districts-Bishnupur and Thoubal under the category of developed districts (score between Mean to Mean + S.D.) and Imphal East and West under the category of highly developed districts (score between Mean + S.D. to 1.00). The status of the districts, thus arrived at, indicates the relative level of development (Fig. 4.2). In absolute term, all the districts of Manipur are below the national standard (T.M. Singh, 1993).

4.3.2 Growth Centre Strategy

For spatial planning in Manipur, ten growth centres-Imphal East (Porompat), Imphal West (Lamphelpat), Thoubal, Bishnupur, Senapati, Tamenglong, Churachandpur, Chandel, Ukhrul and Jiribam form central points for providing socio-economic services and facilities for a larger area than the growth points located in their hinterlands. To mitigate the regional disparities in development in the state, a development strategy based on growth centres, growth points and service centres has been proposed and outlined in relation to the development possibilities in their respective complementary regions.

4.3.2.1 Imphal East (Porompat) Growth Centre

In the hierarchy of central place system in Manipur Imphal stands at the apex by virtue of its enjoying the greatest nodality index forming the growth focus for the entire state and its eastern segment-Porampat growth centre for Imphal East district in the north-eastern part of the central valley. Imphal East planning region, the hinterland of Imphal East (Porompat) growth centre, comprise the service areas of Porompat, Keirao Bitra and Sawombung growth points.

Table 4.3
Disparities in Development in Manipur

Selected economic indicators	Base year	Unit	Imphal	Thoubal	Bishnu-pur	Sena-pati	Tameng-long	Chura-chand-pur	Chandel	Ukhrul	Manipur
1	2	3	4	5	6	7	8	9	10	11	12
Area	1991	km²	1228	514	496	3271	4391	4570	3313	4544	22327
Population	1991	No.	711261	293958	180773	208406	86278	176184	71014	109275	1837149
Fertiliser consumption per 100 ha of cropped area	1991	Tonns.	3.93	7.09	4.45	0.95	0.32	0.55	0.95	0.38	0.03
Tractors per 10000 cultivators	1991	No.	4.58	2.18	2.93	0.26	0.67	0.22	0.82	0.85	1.80
SSI per 1000 population	1991	No.	3.41	0.90	2.02	1.11	2.58	2.12	2.46	5.64	2.55
SSI per 100 km²	1991	No.	196.17	50.58	73.39	7.03	5.03	8.18	5.25	13.64	20.84
Villages electrified	1992	%	100	100	100	81	26	73	72	59	80
Livestock per 100 population	1991	No.	38.74	50.27	62.39	212.40	149.82	56.35	245.61	123.29	82.58
Livestock per km²	1991	No.	223.10	284.02	226.31	134.37	29.20	21.71	52.44	29.83	67.56
Villages covered under water supply	1992	%	72.62	85.71	82.22	73.51	84.90	74.10	69.18	72.52	74.47
Literates to total population	1991	%	59.62	43.66	46.07	43.84	43.84	49.47	37.46	50.25	49.01
Schools per 100 km²	1991	No.	103.75	98.25	68.95	18.83	7.33	13.24	10.05	7.70	19.47
Schools per 1000 population	1991	No.	1.80	1.74	1.90	2.98	3.76	3.44	4.71	3.18	2.38
Teachers per 10000 population	1991	No.	141.50	128.00	111.28	126.18	167.23	147.92	174.17	172.35	139.59

Table 4.3 *(Contd.)*

1	2	3	4	5	6	7	8	9	10	11	12
Teachers per km^2	1991	No.	8.15	7.23	4.04	0.80	0.33	0.57	0.37	0.42	1.14
Doctors per 1000 population	1993	No.	0.27	0.13	0.22	0.15	0.20	0.32	0.42	0.23	0.24
Doctors per 100 km^2	1993	No.	15.64	7.59	8.06	0.98	0.39	1.23	0.91	0.55	1.93
Banks per 100 km^2	1991	No.	3.75	1.95	1.61	0.40	0.09	0.24	0.15	0.11	0.46
Banks per 10000 population	1991	No.	0.65	0.34	0.44	0.63	0.47	0.62	0.71	0.45	0.56
Road length per 100 km^2	1992	km.	97.80	82.88	104.23	21.89	15.77	22.43	15.48	11.76	25.19
Road length per lakh population	1992	km.	169.83	146.70	287.38	346.01	809.10	582.28	809.10	486.04	307.92
Telephone in use per km^2	1987	No.	2.26	0.15	0.12	0.02	0.004	0.03	0.04	0.01	0.15
Telephone in use per 100 population	1987	No.	0.39	0.03	0.03	0.04	0.02	0.08	0.20	0.04	0.18
Weighted Score			0.71	0.40	0.41	0.24	0.26	0.27	0.35	0.28	
Rank			1	3	2	8	7	6	4	5	
Status			Hi. devd.	Devd.	Devd.	Devg.	Devg.	Devg.	Devg.	Devg.	

H. devd. = Highly developed   Devd. = Developed   Devg. = Developing   Mean = 0.37   S.D. = 0.14

Source : Districtwise Development Profile in Manipur.

As the growth focus of the state, Imphal is well poised for its function in so far as the availabaility of the basic infrastructure is concerned. Being the state capital, district and subdivisional headquarters, it is well equipped with the normal administrative infrastructure and enjoys the maximum nodal accessibility. The city possesses the necessary financial, educational, transport, communication and medical institutions (Fig. 4.1) for a take-off in the field of development planning. With only three per cent of the labour force engaged in agriculture and 17 per cent in industries, Imphal has over four-fifths of its working population employed in the tertiary sector.

As the growth focus of the state and growth centre of its immediate neighbourhood, Imphal East has to play its due role in the development of the region. Its functional base has to be strengthened with development of secondary sector-the industries connected with the regional economy, such as dairying, fruit processing, handicrafts and handlooms and agro-based industries which will induce the intensification and diversification of agriculture in the immediate complementary region. With the increased supply of agricultural products from the rural areas the traditional rice, dal and oil mills will naturally be modernised. The diversified intensive agriculture will increase the agricultural productivity and maximise the employment opportunities in the rural sector. The agro-industrial complexes, thus developed at Impahl and other growth centres, will form the core of rural and regional development in Manipur.

In the process of diversification of agriculture, the farmers possessing big landholdings (above 8 ha) and capable of purchasing and utilising modern farm equipments would concentrate on intensive grain farming producing rice, maize, pulses, oilseeds, sugarcane, etc. feeding the grain silos and processing mills. The middle class farmers possessing 2-4 ha of land would utilise farm equipments by hiring them from the cooperatives and big farmers. They may combine dairy farming, horticulture and grain farming with greater emphasis on one or the other depending upon the local conditions and labour strength of their own. The farmers with still smaller holdings (less than 2 ha) may concentrate on vegetable growing with dairy and poultry farming. Thus, everyone connected with agriculture must develop some specialization consistent with the crop rotation requirements, labour availability and scale economies (J. Singh, 1979).

Agro-industrial development will pave the path for the rapid socio-economic transformation and growth of ancillary industries, particularly servicing and manufacture of agricultural implements and variety of consumer goods, which will satisfy the needs of the farmers commensurating to their income growth due to diversification of agriculture. Food processing units, hosiery and readymade garments fabricating plants utilising local handloom products, manufacture of furniture, window and door frames for the houses, sports goods and stationery items will get a boost and will give fillip to the scientific and rational utilisation of resources. Most of these industries will be located at Imphal and other growth centres.

As the demand for better housing facilities will increase immensely with enhanced living standards, two more cement plants-one each in Ukhrul and Chandel districts utilising rich limestone deposits found in these areas, may be established. Similarly, a number of brick manufacturing units, large and small, may be set up along river banks near the central places utilising the huge deposits of sandy clay in the river beds which chock the river channel accentuating the flood hazards in the central valley.

Fig. 4.3 shows the pattern of agricultural specialisation-diversification visualised on the basis of existing traits and emerging trends and on the assumption of the creation of the necessary infrastructure outlined in the preceding sections. A brief analysis of the agro-industrial diversification is presented taking the complmentary regions of each growth point and their constituent service centres.

Porompat growth point, with four service centres-Thongju, Kshetrigao, Heingang and Koirengei, has a service area comprising

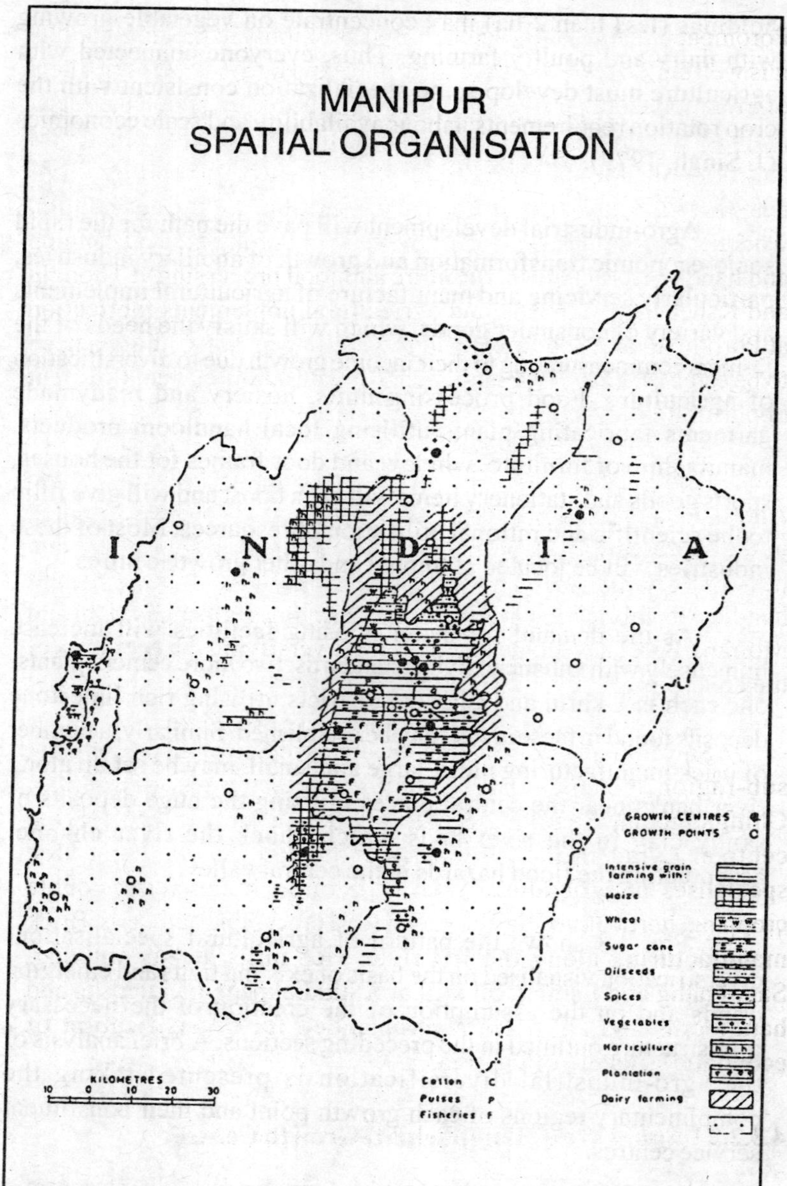
MANIPUR
SPATIAL ORGANISATION
I N D I A
GROWTH CENTRES
GROWTH POINTS
Intensive grain farming with:
Maize
Wheat
Sugar cane
Oilseeds
Spices
Vegetables
Horticulture
Plantation
Dairy farming
KILOMETRES
10 0 10 20 30
Cotton C
Pulses P
Fisheries F

Fig. 4.3

Porompat planning sub-region. For its proximity to the state capital, it is well suited to develop dairy farming and horticulture. With help of irrigation facilities, being extended to the area by Thoubal project, double cropping will become a possibility. Sugarcane, vegetables and oilseeds may be introduced to the area as supporting crops besides rice to enhance the income generation of the agricultural workers. Agricultural extension services at Porompat, fruit canning and handicrafts at Andro, furniture and food processing at Thongju and Kshetrigao, dairying and agricultural implements fabrication at Porompat, and handloom and saw milling at Top Chingtha need to be established and strengthened to create additional employment opportunities and economic face-lift of the area.

Keirao Bitra growth point covers the service areas of Tulihal Andro, Changamdabi and Moirang Purel service centres, situated in the south-east of Imphal, the area specialises in agriculture and horticulture. The food processing at Tulihal, handloom and handicrafts fabrication at Andro, and dairying at Changamdabi and Moirang Purel have to be taken up for diversifying the economy of the area.

Sawombung growth point, the focus of Sawombung planning sub-region, consists of the complementary areas of Lamlai, Chingangbam, Sagolmang, Khundrakpam and Laikot service centres. Lying in the north-east of Imphal, Sawombung area specialises in agriculture. With little effort it can adopt double cropping, horticulture, dairying, and food processing activities. Brick manufacturing along the Iril river, rice mills at Sawombung, Sagolmang and Lamlai, oil mill at Khundrakpam, handicrafts and handlooms at Laikot are recommended for diversification of economic structure of the area.

4.3.2.2 Imphal West (Lamphelpat) Growth Centre

The hinterland of Imphal West (Lamphelpat) growth centre covers the service areas of Lamphelpat, Lamsang, Patsoi and Wangoi growth points. Imphal West (Lamphelpat) serves as the growth pole for the entire state growth centre for the district and growth point for its urban hinterland. Beyond the urban zone of Imphal city, the district is endowed with fertile alluvial plain with rich forest wealth on its north and western outskirts and as such is well suited for further diversification of its agro-industrial economy.

Lamphelpat growth point serves the complementary areas of Iroisemba and Naoriya Pakhanglakpa service centres located on the western margin of the city. The area is highly urbanized and industrialized. Takyel industrial estate, located in the area, accommodates a large number of small scale industries, electronics to cycle manufacturing.

Lamsang growth point commands the service areas of Sekmai, Kanglatongbi, Khonghampat, Phayeng and Mayang Langjing service centres. With the first spinning mill of the state situated in the area at Loitang Khunou and the first industrial growth centres coming up at Kanglatongbi, the region is well poised to develop industries at an impressive scale for its nearness to the resource rich forest-clad hills. Sekmai and Khonghampat can develop modern rice mills, Kanglatongbi wood and fruit processing industries, Phayeng and Mayang Langjing food-processing and handicrafts. In agricultural diversification cotton, sugarcane and horticulture can be introduced in the crop culture with help of recently extended irrigation facilities. Double cropping of rice can be taken up in larger parts of this region.

Patsoi growth point serves the complimentary areas of Konthoujam, Lamjaotongba, Maisnam Kangmong and Maklang service centres. Comprising the fertile agricultural tracts, the region can develop rice mills at Konthoujam and Maklang, handlooms and handicrafts at Lamjaotongba and horticulture and lumbering at Maisnam Kangmong for its proximity to the forest clad hills.

Wangoi planning sub-region with Wangoi as growth point embraces the service areas of Mayang Imphal, Lilong Chajing, Samurou, Mongsangei, Hiyangthang and Kodompokpi service centres. For its location between the Loktak lake and the Imphal river and with extension of irrigation facilities from Imphal barrage, the area has made a marked progress in agricultural and horticultural production. Double-cropping of rice, vegetables including potato, poultry farming, pisciculture and horticulture have made headway in the region and need further intensification by use of labour and inputs. Lilong Chajing for wood processing, Mongsangei, Hiyangthang, Kodompokpi and Samurou for agro-processing, Mayang Imphal for consumer goods and tourism, and Wangoi for an industrial growth centre are well suited.

4.3.2.3 Thoubal Growth Centre

The complementary region of Thoubal growth centre comprises the service areas of Thoubal, Lilong and Kakching growth points. Thoubal, thus, serves as the growth centre for the entire district and as growth point for its immediate hinterland. With fertile alluvial plain, assured irrigation facilities, proximity to Imphal and the forest and mineral rich hills in the east, the region is well set to agro-industrial diversification and intensification. The northern part of the region is the most important vegetable growing area of the state while the southern part forms the rice bowl of the valley feeding a much larger population than its own. Agricultural research centre at Wangbal has helped in introducing improved seeds and techniques while the sugar khandsari factory at Khangabok has provided impetus to the sugarcane growers. The lakes and wetlands of the district form important fishing grounds and add to the scenic beauty which alongwith historic monuments form important tourist attractions.

Thoubal growth point commanding the service areas of Khongjom, Heirok, Yairipok, Sikhong Sekmai and Wangjing service centres has better prospects for agricultural diversification and development of agro-based industries. The area has great scope for the transformation of agricultural structure into a predominantly horticultural and animal based economy by itensifying vegetable and fruit farming, dairying, poultry raising and pisciculture. Sugarcane cultivation in Khongjom and Yairipok, and intensive grain farming in Wangjing and Sikhong Sekmai areas may be taken up at enhanced scale. Agro- and forest based industries-rice and dal mills, saw mills, mat making, pottery, salt making, handicrafts and handlooms have bright prospects in the region. Brick manufacturing may be taken up near Thoubal and Yairipok to utilise the sandy clay available in Thoubal river bed.

Lilong growth point serves the hinterlands of Haoreibi, Leisangthem, Moijing and Irong Chesaba service centres which have rich horticultural base, and as such can develop agro-based industries along the National Highway 39, which passes through this region. For its location in the inter-riverine tract, Lilong area can develop riverine fisheries in Iril and Imphal river courses besides specialising in poultry and handicrafts at Haoreibi and Leisangthem and pisciculture and horticulture at Irong Chesaba and Moijing. Lilong, an important market town, can develop food processing industries besides horticulture and poultry farming.

Kakching growth point has six service centres-Kakching Khunou, Wabgai, Sugnu, Hiyanglam, Langmeidong and Pallel in its complementary region, where intensive agriculture with double cropping of rice is well poised for diversification. Horticulture, vegetable culture, sugarcane cultivation, pisciculture, poultry and dairy farming can be introduced in the agricultural economy of the region to increase the job opportunities in the rural sector besides enhancing the agricultural productivity and income. Modern rice mills can be established at Kakching while food processing units at Wabgai, Hiyanglam and Langmeidong and manufacture of consumer goods at Pallel can be taken up economically to boost the regional economy. Sugnu near the confluence of Chakpi and Manipur rivers have immense prospects for tourism and allied activities. Based on rice straw a paper board plant can be started at Kakching Khunou. A milk processing plant, if established at Pallel, will boost the lot of cattle graziers living in its vicinity. Handlooms and handicrafts sector has to be popularised in all the service centres of the region to generate more employment opportunities and better income to the people engaged in these activities. In the depressed parts- with lake water pisciculture can be taken up on scientific lines.

4.3.2.4 Bishnupur Growth Centre

The hinterland of this growth centre is located between the Loktak lake and foothills of the Manipur western hills and comprise the service areas of Bishnupur, Nambol and Moirang growth points. The space economy of this planning region is marked by intensive cultivation, pisciculture, handicrafts and tourism, Being the district, subdivisional and block headquarters, Bishnupur is well equipped with the normal administrative paraphernalia and possesses the necessary financial, educational, transport, communication and medical facilities and services giving a helping hand in the developmental planning of the region. Bishnupur, as such, has to play its due role in the development of the district as a whole in general and the Bishnupur block, for which it is the growth point, in particular, which forms its zone of influence.

Bishnupur growth point has a service area covering the complementary areas of Nachou, Ningthoukhong, Ngaikhong Khullen, Phubala and Keinou service centres. The town can have an agro-industrial complex with dairy, poultry and fruit processing units besides the rice and dal mills. Cottage industries-handlooms, handicrafts, mat making and stone works have to be developed on cooperative lines to make them more remunerative, attractive and job generating activities. The off shore areas of the lake can go for intensive pisciculture and afforestation. Double and multiple-cropping with rice, pulses, sugarcane, vegetables including potato and orchard farming have to be introduced in the crop culture of the area to improve the economic relevance of this sector in generation of ample income and employment. Processing of agricultural products may be taken up at Ningthoukhong, while stress should be given to intensify handloom weaving and handicrafts at Keinou.

Nambol growth point serves the hinterlands of Oinam, Utlou, Leimapokpam and Irengbam service centres. Nambol is a developing township between Imphal and Bishnupur which has specialised in agricultural marketing. The state government has planned a sugar mill at Kabowakching on the outskirts of Nambol. Oinam and Utlou service centres have to develop agricultural processing units and vagetable gardening, while Leimapokpam and Irengbam should develop handicrafts and handlooms besides horticulture and intensive farming.

Moirang growth point serves the complementary areas of Thanga, Kwakta, Kumbi, Wangoo and Saiton service centres in addition to that of its own. Moirang is the subdivisional and block headquarters, seat of an old principality, an important educational and business centre and the most important tourist spot for its historic monuments and attractive lake view. As growth point, the town must have greater accent on the tertiary sector rather than secondary. Tourism, transport, repairing workshops, trade and commerce form base of the economic structure of Moirang. The town is well suited to develop fish processing plants, manufacture of paper and card boards and agro-processing units for its central location on the converging point of transport routes. Thanga and Moirang service centre areas will concentrate on intensive pisciculture and tourism for their locational advantages in the Loktak region in the vicinity of Keibul Lamjao game sancturary. Kwakta, Wangoo and Saiton will be able to develop rice mills as their hinterlands will adopt multiple cropping pattern and diversification of agriculture by taking up poultry, piggery and dairying. These economic activities will give impetus to employment generation and income augmentation in the rural sector.

4.3.2.5 Senapati Growth Centre

Covering the northern hill tracts of the state, this growth centre serves the complementary areas of Tadubi, Paomata, Pural, Saikul Kangpokpi and Saitu growth points besides the service area of its own. Characterised with thick forests, shifting cultivation intermixed with terrace cultivation, horticulture and dairying this region has the lowest proportion of its population living below the poverty line but lacks in infrastructure (Fig. 4.1). Being the district headquarters and seat of autonomous district council, Senapati is a fast developing centre with increasing proportion of tertiary sector workers. With adequate infrastructure it is well set to develop its busines activities, social facilities and services for the improvement of living standards of the people.

Tadubi growth point serves the service areas of Mao Songsong, Makhan Centre, Punanamei, Yangkhullen, Maram and Tinsong service centres. Forest clad hills and rich fertile terraces in this planning sub-region are well suited for agro-industrial intensification and diversification. Rice, potato, maize and orchard growing need further intensification. Wood, fruit and agro processing units will further the economic lot of the people-mainly Mao and Maram Nagas. Their artistic culture, superb loinloom products, fancy handicrafts all have bearing on economic transformation of the region. Wood processing-saw milling, furniture and small paper plants can be established at Karong, Maram and Mao Songsong, and handicrafts and handloom/loinloom weaving at Makhan, Punanamei and Tiinsong to generate income and empolyment to the people. Yangkhullen may undertake timber logging and handicrafts, and Mao Songsong tourism on a grand scale.

Paomata growth point embraces the service areas of Tunggam Khullen, Liyai Khullen and Laii service centres. All these centres have to develop timber processing and weaving besides agricultural diversification with stress on horticulture, orchard farming, poultry and dairying.

Purul growth point covers the hinterlands of Oinam, Phaibung Khullen, Khongdei Khuman and Thingba Khunou service centres, which are well suited to develop forest-based industries besides loinloom weaving, horticulture, agriculture, poultry and piggery.

The complementary region of Saikul growth point covers the service areas of Laikoiching, Thangal Surung, Leitanpokpi, Thangkangphai and Phunam Maring service centres, all of them having population below 1000. Peopled by Nepalese, Nagas and Kukis, this region is well suited to diversification of agriculture-cultivation of rice, maize and vegetables alongwith rabi crops-wheat, mustard and peas, dairying, poultry and piggery. A milk processing plant and an oil mill can be started at Saikul. Saw milling and handlooms are recommended for other centres.

The service zone of Kangpokpi growth point covers the hinterlands of Keithalmanbi, Kalapahar and Chalwa service centres. Inhabited by Kukis and Nepalese, this area is marked by a space economy comprising intensive cultivation with rice, maize, vegetables and fruits, dairying, piggery and poultry, wood processing and rice milling. Kangpokpi as the subdivisional, block and autonomous district headquarters has sufficient infrastructural support to develop secondary and tertiary sectors. Milk processing and fruit canning plants may be set up at Kangpokpi and wood processing units may be established at Keithalmanbi and Kalapahar. A corn flakes unit is recommended for Kalapahar.

Along the foothills overlooking the valley lies Saitu growth point, which covers the service areas of Motbung, Leimakhong and Kangchup. With Kukis and Nepalese inhabiting the area, there is ample scope for the development of dairying, horticulture, piggery and poultry in the area along with loinloom weaving, pottery and cane work.

4.3.2.6 Tamenglong Growth Centre

Within the complementary region of Tamenglong growth centre lies the service areas of Tousem, Tamei and Nungba growth points alongwith the service area of its own. Covering the northern half of the western hill tracts, this region has poor connectivity and accordingly low level of development. The region has a rich natural resource base consisting of the lush green forests in the Barak drainage with famous bamboo stands, swift-flowing streams, optimum climate for tea and orchard farming and favourable slopes for hill cultivation. Tamenglong, in the heart of the planning region, is the district, subdivisional and block headquarters and as such generates and provides growth impulses to all the central places in the district, more particularly to its immediate hinterland comprising the service areas of Marangjing, Akhui, Haochong, Shongphel Khunou and Awangkhul. The depressed economy of the area due to lack of marketing and transport infrastructure can get a boost by reorganisation of the space economy in a planned manner. A programme of agro-industrial diversification can effectively check the downward trend of economy. The shifting cultivation has to be replaced by terrace cultivation in a phased manner. The abandoned Jhumlands can be brought under horticulture, particularly orchard farming for growing oranges, banana and pineapple, and plantations-tea and coffee, for which the region has excellent ecological conditions. A fruit processing plant at Tamenglong and dairying and handicrafts units at Akhui and Awangkhul are recommended. Bamboo and cane works can be taken up at other centres.

Tousem growth point serves the hinterlands of old Magulong, Thiulon, Oinamlong and Namtiram service centres, Due to poor linkage this region is not able to utilise its rich forest resources comprising quality canes and bamboos. With proper water management, for its location in between Jiri and Barak rivers, Tousem can develop double cropping along the river beds and in the terraced fields. Besides rice, potato, vegetables, fruits, dairying and poultry farming have bright prospects under the agricultural diversification programme. With its scenic beauty and waterfalls tourism can be planned to boost the economic lot of the people by opening the area, for which road links have to be provided both from Tamenglong as well as Jiribam. Even ropeways can link Tousem with Tamenglong, which in itself will be a tourist attraction. Rice mills at Tousem, Oinamlong and Namtiram and poultry and piggery farms for Old Magulong and Thiulon are recommended.

In the complementary region of Tamei growth point, comprising the service areas of Langmei, Kadi, Lenglong, Chaton and Lenta service centres agro-forestry sector can be developed to give a boost to the space economy. Large scale jhuming prevalent in the area have to be gradually replaced by terrace cultivation and the jhumlands are to be brought under horticulture. Dairying and poultry farming can be taken up on intensive scale alongwith stress on weaving and handicrafts. Maize and oilseeds can be grown in the area alongwith rice to improve the economic fortunes of agricultural workers.

Nungba planning sub-region for its location on the National Highway 53 between Imphal West and Jiribam growth centres is well suited to diversify its agro-forestry sector by introducing double cropping in the Khoupum valley and along the river beds. Nungba growth point being the subdivisional and block headquarters, provides services and facilities to the service areas of Khoupum Chingthak, Noney, Dolang, Lubanglong and Nungnang service centres. Khoupum Chingthak and Noney may concentrate on agricultural processing and dairying while other centres can take up bamboo and cane fabrication to augment economic prospects of the rural-tribal population. Nungba area can take up tea plantation alongwith orchard farming besides a small fruit canning unit located at the growth point.

4.3.2.7 Churachandpur Growth Centre

Within the complementary region of Churachandpur growth centre there are five other growth points of Parbung, Thanlon, Henglep, Samulamlan and Singngat. The larger chunk of population living in its immediate neighbourhood is served by the growth centre itself. The town. thus, forms the growth point for Saikot, Mata, Thingkangphai, Teiseng, Lhangbung (Geljang) and Gangpimaul service centres and growth centre for the entire district. The area has already specialised in chillies and ginger farming besides rice cultivation. With assured irrigation, after completion of the Khuga barrage, it can intensify the agricultural operations by adopting double and multiple-cropping with major emphasis on commercial farming of spices and vegetables. To utilise the natural and agricultural resources, agro-forestry processing units like saw milling, furniture and stationery, rice and oil mills can be started at Churachandpur, Saikot and Mata. Other service centres may take up poultry, dairying, weaving and handicrafts fabrication besides stress on intensive cultivation on favourable slopes.

Samulamlan growth point has a service area comprising hinterlands of Sagang, Ngariyan, Keirap Khunthak and Khoirentak Khunou service centres. For its proximity to Churachandpur and Moirang towns this area has to concentrate on horticulture and poultry. Vegetables in the Khuga basin and fruits and poultry farming on the foothills may be taken up on impressive scale. Handloom weaving and handicrafts fabrication based on indigenous skill will prove immensely helpful in raising the income of the tribal people alongwith their living standards. Rice milling at Sagang and tourism promotion of Khoirentak may be taken up for the economic diversification of the space economy.

The service zone of Parbung growth point includes the service areas of Senvon, Pherzawl, Tinsuong, Patpuimun, Tipaimukh (Sipuikon) and Sibapurikhal service centres. The rich forest cover and river beds of Barak and Tuivai offer development potential for forest-based industries and agricultural diversification. Parbung-Tipaimukh area is quite suitable for dairying and orchard farming, Senvon, Sibapurikhal and Pherzawl for saw milling, and Tinsuong and Patpuimun for weaving and crafts, which may be taken up as means to ameliorate the economic lot of the people. The jhuming, widley practised in the area, has to be replaced by terrace cultivation in a phased manner without distrubing the tribal economy.

The hinterland of Thanlon growth point covering the service areas of Bukpi, Mualnuam, Suangsang, Leijangaphai and Kaihlam has conditions similar to those of Parbung and accordingly can adopt a mixed economy-intensive cultivation along river beds and terraces with rice, pulses and vegetables, poultry and piggery and saw milling. Thanlon and Bukpi should have rice and saw mills while other centres may concentrate on agricultural intensification, poultry and orchard farming.

Henglep growth point and its hinterland, formed of the service areas of Santing, Vungbuk, Charoi Khullen, S. Nabil and Lhengjang service centres, is the most backward tract of the district. The region has very poor connectivity and low pace of growth. Forestry and agricultural sectors have to be developed to improve the economy. Systematic exploitation of forest wealth and agricultural diversification by introducing fruit and vegetable cultivation besides poultry and piggery have to be taken up in right earnest. Rice milling and crafts centre may be established at Henglep to give an economic face-lift to the area. Other centres should concentrate on tribal arts and crafts to enhance income of the people in the rural sector.

Singngat growth point, located to the south of Churachandpur, serves the hinterlands of Behiang, Suvangdoh, Muallum, Kangkap and Lungchin service centres. Intensive cultivation with the help of assured irriagation from Khuga barrage will enhance the prospects of diversification of rural economy in this region. Besides double cropping of rice and spices-chillies and ginger the area, will be able to raise orchards, vegetables, poultry and piggery. Singngat and Behiang can support rice mills and other centres may specialise in weaving, horticulture and poultry farming. The scenic beauty along the Tiddim Road connecting Imphal with Tiddim town in Myanmar can be exploited for promotion of tourism.

4.3.2.8 Chandel Growth Centre

This growth centre has better prospects of development than the others, except Imphal because it has within its complementary region a wider variety of resources-the narrow fertile river valleys, rich minerals-limestones and chromite, economically valuable forests with teak and pine trees and good linkage with the central valley and the fertile Kabaw valley of Myanmar. Chandel growth centre serves the service areas of Moreh, Machi and Chakpikarong service centres alongwith its own service area, which consists of the hinterlands of Lambung, Liwa Khullen, Komlathabi, Khudei Khunou, Larong and Tonsen Khullen service centres. Chandel, with district level infrastructure, has good scope to develop secondary sector-forest based and agro-based industries like saw milling, rice mills, match manufacturing, consumer goods and food processing units. Komlathabi and Lambung can develop rice mills and other centres poultry, dairying and weaving units besides intensification of agriculture by introducing double cropping, orchard farming and horticulture.

Moreh growth point ecompasses the service areas of Tengnoupal, Narum, Aimol Khullen, Leibi and Chalsam Tengnoupal service centres. For its rich mineral resources and gregarious forest wealth a mini-cement plant at Khudengthabi near Moreh and timber processing plants at Moreh will be economically viable and physically feasible. Other service centres can have handloom and handicrafts units, poultry, piggery and horticulture with pineapple and vegetable farming. Moreh, a flourishing town on Indo-Myanmar border, which commands international trade between our two countries, is bound to be an important centre with a number of industries-food processing, servicing, consumer goods, milk and fruit processing.

Machi growth point covers the service areas of Lamlong Khullen, Tollen, Khoibu and Kangshang service centres. The forest wealth and scenic hills in the area have immense tourist potential. The service centres as such can be developed as tourist spots besides development of horliculture, piggery, poultry, handlooms and handicrafts.The area around Kangshang is well suited for development of agriculture and horticulture.

In the hinterland of Chakpikarong growth point lies the service areas of Khubung Khunou, New Somtal, Molcham, Sugnu Lamhang, Khongkang Sawompa and Haika service centres. Dotted with rich forests, this region has not been able to utilise its natural resources for poor linkage. With development of road network, it can very well undertake programmes for economic diversification by setting up saw mills and wood based industries in almost all the service centres alongwith poultry, piggery and orchard farming to boost the local economy.

4.3.2.9 Ukhrul Growth Centre

The hinterland of Ukhrul growth centre covers the service

regions of Chingai, Kasom Khullen, Kamjong and Phungyar growth points in addition to that of its own. With lush-green forests dominated by pine trees, rich limestone and chromite deposits and swift flowing rivers, the region is well set to diversify its economic structure by opening industrial units and creating agricultural complexes supported by orchard farming, dairying, poultry and piggery besides intensive grain farming over the terraced landscape.

The service region of Ukhrul growth point, comprising the complementary areas of Hundung, Tolloi, Tuinem, Khamasom and Mapum service centres, for its central location with medium conectivity, is eminently suited for agricultural diversification and industrial development. The jhumlands have to be gradually brought under horticulture-fruit and vegetable cultivation and dairying. Poultry and piggery have good prospects in almost all the settlements. Intensive agriculture should be practised on the terraced and favourable slopes. Hundung, which has a mini-cement plant can have a tile factory, Tolloi and Tuinem modern rice mills, Sanakeithal and Khamasom wood industries and Mapum handlooms and handicrafts. Ukhrul in the vicinity of Khankhui limestone caves and Siroi hill with famous rock lily is well poised for development of tourism as a major sector of economy.

Chingai growth point serves the complementary areas of Chingjaroi, Paoyi, Jessami, Kharasom, New Tusom and Paorei service centres. With rich forest wealth and fertile river beds a programme of agro-industrial diversification can be taken up to transform the economy of this region. Agricultural sector needs augmentation by introducing poultry, piggery, handlooms and handicrafts in the rural sector. Rice and saw mills at Jessami and Paoyi, food processing unit at Chingai and handicrafts at other centres are recommended to be established to improve the local economy and living standards of the people by enhancing their income and consumption levels.

Kasom Khullen growth point has a complementary region consisting the service areas of Nambashi, Mawai, Khamlang,

Nongdam and Kangkuk, which is characterised with distressed economy. A programme of agricultural diversification by introducing poultry, horticulture and intensive cultivation in favourable areas can mitigate the poverty of the region. Rice and saw mills are recommended at Kasom Khullen while all the service centres have to concentrate on agriculture, horticulture and livestock rearing for augmenting their economy.

The hinterland of Kamjong growth point includes the service areas of Ningthi, Chatrik Khullen, Grihang, Maku, Nampisha and Chamu service centres with agro-economic conditions similar to Kasom Khullen. The region, accordingly, has to take up similar economic activities like orchard farming, livestock rearing and cultivation of vegetables alongwith rice and oilseeds on the lower slopes and river beds. Rice and saw mills at Kamjong, rice mills at Ningthi and Chatrik Khullen and handlooms and handicrafts at other centres are recommended.

Phungyar growth point serves the hinterlands of Thawai, Sekibung, Lungphu, Chadong, Sorbung and Phalang service centres. The region has almost similar conditions as prevalent in Kamjong and Kasom Khullen areas. Agricultural diversification with introduction of maize and potato in the crop culture alongwith rice, poultry and piggery on intensive scale and horticulture on the abandoned jhums will boost the economic lot of the people. Rice mills at Phungyar, Sekibung and Thawai and saw mills at Chadong, Lungphu and Sorbung, and poultry and dairying at Phalang can be taken up as part of the economic diversification programme to contain poverty in the area.

4.3.2.10 Jiribam Growth Centre

Jiribam growth centre occupies a central position on the National Highway 53 between Imphal and Silchar and commands the road and river links to Tousem and Nungba in Tamenglong district and Tipaimukh in Churachandpur district. It is the only growth centre of the state having links with the rail network in the country. Serving the hinterlands of Hilghat, Latingkhal, Jakuradhor, Sonapur, Borobekra and Boroikhal service centres, Jiribam is perhaps the most prospective development centre in Manipur with its vast natural resource base-the rich forests in the neighbourhood, Jiri-Barak water ways, the fertile soils, levelled land and optimum ecological conditions for tea, coffee and rubber plantations besides the locational advantages.

The region is well suited for agro-industrial intensification and diversification. Introduction of double and multiple cropping pattern with rice, wheat, mustard, pulses, spices-ginger, chillies, vegetables, particularly potato, beans and brinjal and fruits-mango, jackfruit, papaya and banana can generate ample employment and income to the people living in its hinterland. Plantation crops-tea, rubber, cardamom, lemon and coffee have already been introduced in the area and have prospects for further intensification.

A bamboo-chipping plant has already been set up to utilise rich bamboo stands found in the Manipur western hills. It can be developed into a full-fledged paper mill. A tea factory and rubber processing plant can be established at Jiribam to utilise the locally produced tea leaves and rubber. A fruit canning plant can be commissioned in this growth centre to boost the lot of the horticulturists and fruit growers. Rice and saw mills can be set up at all the service centres of the region. Jiribam can also be developed as a tourist centre for its scenic environs and superb location with efficient transport system.

4.4 Conclusion

Inspite of the change in the priorities during the successive Five Year Plans, the state has not been able to achieve a balanced socio-economic development. Even in the sectors like agriculture, in which Manipur was self sufficient in the past, could not keep the pace with the requirements of growing population. Same is true with almost all sectors of development. In the light of the prevalent situation, schemes and proposals for sectoral and spatial planning of the state have been enunciated for a period of ten years or so in this part of the study. Enough stress is laid in these programmes on the construction and maintenance of infrastructures-transport and communication, financial institutions and marketing and social facilities, alongwith the intensification, diversification and commercialization of agriculture. The agro based industries suggested therein will bring further intensification of agriculture. Much more emphasis on agriculture and allied activities will prove to be instrumental in elimination of poverty, unemployment and under-employment from the face of the state. The planning proposals for transformation of the hill economy like gradual replacement of jhuming by terrace cultivation, introduction of horticulture in the abandoned jhumlands, stress on indigenous crafts, forest-based industries, dairying, poultry and piggery will generate enough employment and income to the hill people. As marketing of the products from the hill region has to be done in the valley, an integration in the hill and valley economy will be achieved. Thus, the programmes under sectoral and spatial frames suggested herein will bring an integrated approach to the planned development and socio-economic transformation of the state.

5

Summary And Conclusion

Planning in India is largely concerned with the balanced development of areas and people. As such, since its inception, planning has been dynamic in its approach to develop regions and achieve social justice for the people. About five decades of planned development has resulted in unequal development of regions and growing social tensions. As a remedial measure to this phenomena, problem regions such as backward areas, hill areas, drought prone areas and flood affected areas were given special consideration in the successive Five Year Plans. Despite special plans and budgets, the problems faced by these regions remained partially unsolved. The recent trend observed therein is the faster rate of outward mobility of manpower and resources from these regions. Siphoning of natural resources, on the one hand, and of active working population, on the other, augments poverty and cements backwardness in these areas. Leakage of natural resources from the backward regions of the country leaves limited scope behind for regional development. It is in this context that a study relating to assessment of the role of various plans and their implementation becomes imperative and important.

The present study is an exercise towards application to techniques of integrated regional development to the socio-economic development of Manipur, a small hill state in North East India. The study rests upon certain basic principles of integrated area development and also some specific aims and objectives. It confines itself to the task of identification of growth centres and their hinterlands, resource appraisal and pinpointing the location of development potential in each sector of economy, a step towards future comprehensive planning. The specific characteristic of the study region and the appraisal of its natural, economic and cultural resources was considered necessary to be analysed first of all, which has helped in the demarcation of the planning regions and in recommending future programmes for regional development.

Manipur can broadly be divided into three natural regions- the Manipur hills, the Manipur valley and the Barak basin. The hills, which cover about nine-tenths of the state area, comprise five districts of Senapati, Tamenglong, Churachandpur, Chandel and Ukhrul, accommodating over one-third of the state population. The valley, on the other hand, with only nine per cent of the state area, shelters about two-thirds of the state population in four districts of Imphal East, Imphal West, Thoubal and Bishnupur. The tiny Barak basin, a riverine plain on the western margin of the state, is tagged with Imphal East district for administrative purposes.

About 27.52 per cent of the state population live in the towns numbering 31, and the rest 72.48 per cent in 2,182 villages, organised into 39 community/tribal development blocks.

With predominantly tribal population, shifting agricultural economy, absence of industries and least of urbanisation, the hill districts of Manipur present a scene of poverty, unemployment, economic exploitation, social deprivation, poor health, illiteracy and lack of infrastructure. As such, it is difficult to think of the balanced development of the state without improving lot of the tribal people living in the hill districts.

The state by its topographical structure had problems of economic development and socio-economic transformation for a pretty long period. Manipur presents a true picture of the conditions prevailing in the scarcity pockets of the Indian economy. The low per capita income, a fast increasing population, absence of industries, huge but mostly unskilled manpower are the familiar contours of this economically backward and depressed region. The economic stagnation of the state has led 45 per cent of her people to live a life below the poverty line.

The study primarily rests upon two types of integration-spatial and functional, which are in themselves interrelated in the process of development. Functional integration of various sectors such as agriculture, horticulture, industry, infrastructure and so on has been suggested by making use of a spatial model, in which development in one sector opens up possibilities for the development in another. The spatial relationship among various socio-economic activities depends a great deal on where they are located. It is found that activities often cluster in hierarchical pattern in space.

The spatial model used for these two levels of integration is founded on carefully selected planning units at various hierarchic levels, which is based on the fact that development in a region does not take place without any pattern, rather the space is organised in a definite system. This concept has been expressed in the theory of growth centre planning, a modified form of the theories of Von Thunen, Christaller and Losch, and later expanded by Boudeville and Perroux. The first task in a growth centre planning has, therefore, been to identify the focal points of growth, which will be centrally located within their service area and will be functionally linked with the dependent settlements for various activities.

The focal points (central places) have been identified on the basis of their functional establishments and centrality. In the present study, nine district headquarters-Imphal East (Porompat), Imphal West (Lamphelpat), Thoubal, Bishnupur, Senapati and Tamenglong, Churachandpur, Chandel and Ukhrul besides Jiribam, a block headquarter on the western outskirts of the state, have been identified as growth centres, and the sub-divisional/block headquarters as growth points, mainly for their policy functions. In the growth centres and growth points are located the propulsive firms-the developmental infrastructure and institutions, which exert a strong influence over their surroundings and which are capable of generating sustained growth over a long period of time.

Each growth point has been supported by varying number of service centres selected on the basis of their centrality score. The hinterlands or the service areas of the growth centres and growth points are delineated on the basis of district and block boundaries and that of the service centres on the basis of Reilly's Retail Gravitational Model, determining the functional relationship between a central place and its dependent settlements.

The service areas of the growth centres termed as planning regions, of the growth points as planning sub regions and of the service centres as basic planning units, have been taken into account for the allocation of different economic activities, such as the basic planning units for the provision of lower order social facilites and economic infrastructure to develop agricultural sector, planning sub-regions for other higher order functions and infrastructure, and the planning regions for development of industries, higher social facilities and infrasturctures like transport, irrigation etc.

The integrated regional development programme is a multi-level, multi-sector and multi-section concept. Obviously, it encompasses rural development (i) at various levels in spatial hierarchy such as viable cluster of villages, block and district, (ii) at various sectors/sub-sectors of rural economy such as agriculture, industry, education, health, transport etc., and (iii) at various poorer sections of rural population such as landless labourers, artisans, small and marginal farmers, scheduled castes and scheduled tribes, etc. The integrated regional development plan, thus, has got the thrust in the framework of block level planning, which is to be fitted into a hierarchy of levels both above and below.

The implementation of economic development programmes in the successive Five Year Plans has led to disparity between agriculture and non-agricultural sectors and between different regions and different sections of the society besides decline in employment in traditional crafts and industries and degradation of environment and natural resource base. As such, planning proposals for integrated regional development have been formulated and presented in the sectoral and spatial frame for the modernisation and growth of space economy in the state.

Agriculture, being the mainstay of the population, assumes pivotal role in the regional development. The problem of agricultural development in the state is the problem of introducing improved cropping patterns, improved techniques and maximising inputs of resources in agriculture. Accordingly it is proposed for the possible adjustments in agricultural landuses, land development programme, reorientation in cropping patterns including diversification of crops, development of irrigation facilities, adoption of measures for soil conservation and flood control, and provision of agricultural support services to make agriculture more remunerative and attractive sector of economy. In the allied sector, measures have been suggested to raise the quality of livestock, poultry and other animals, to augment the production of fish and development of pisciculture, and utilisation of vast forest resources.

The problem of industrial development in the state is the problem of developing agro- and forest-based industries to utilise the available resources in the region and its neighbourhood. As such, it is recommended for assured supply of raw materials and marketing network for the handloom and handicrafts sector, development of resource-based industries including fruit canning, dairy and paper besides an intensive programme for industrial training to attract youths towards small and tiny sector industries aiming at the larger share of employment in this sector.

The state in general and the hills in particular lack in infrastructural facilities, adversely affecting the socio-economic development. As such, a concerted effort has to be made to develop transport, communication, power, education, medical and health, veterinary and marketing facilities for the social well-being of the people. It is, therefore, proposed that all the service centres be linked with growth points, the block headquarters, and the growth points with the growth centres, the district headquarters, by all-weather metalled roads, while the villages should be provided effective linkage with the service centres. Rail and river transport have to be extended and reoriented to the needs of the region. A large section of the rural population lacks communication facilities. Therefore, more post offices are proposed in the hill areas. Educational, medical and health, and veterinary facilities have to be qualitatively improved to provide better services to the people. It is, therefore, proposed to construct/ repair buildings of educational institutions, medical, health and veterinary centres besides equipping them with qualified personnel and amenities. More educational institutions, health and veterinary centres/sub-centres have accordingly been proposed to improve the quality of life. The hill areas also lack marketing and banking facilities and the people have to travel long distances for consumer goods. As such, proposals have been made to establish new markets and open bank branches in the hill districts.

The service centres and growth points in the hill districts bave to concentrate on primary activities-agriculture and forestry in the process of economic development and the growth centres on the development of forest and agro-based industries. Tamenglong growth centre, with large scale production of oranges, can develop fruit canning industry on an impressive scale, while Ukhrul growth centre is well suited for mineral based industries for the rich limestones and chromite found in the neighbourhood.

Imphal East and West growth centres are ideally located for the development of tertiary activities, while Thoubal and Bishnupur growth centres, and Kakching and Moirang growth points can have more industrial establishments using the raw materials from the neighbouring hill areas. Jiribam growth centre in the Barak basin is well poised for an industrial breakthrough for its vast natural resource base.

The service centres in the valley in the vicinity of the Loktak lake will continue to concentrate on fisheries alongwith agriculture, while other service centres in the valley, are well poised to develop agriculture alongwith handicrafts, including the handlooms.

As the development of one sector opens up the possibilities for another, the development activities under various administrative departments have to be coordinated with each other. Interlinking of one spatial unit with another will help to achieve a comprehensive development of the region by optimum utilisation of locally available resources. Thus, the spatial and functioal integration will ensure a balanced and overall development of the region.

The present study, thus, provides some insight into the emerging patterns of space relations and settlement hierarchy of a fascinating region. It is hoped that the model of sectoral and spatial planning enunciated in the study in reference to the available resources, if implemented in right perspective, will bring desired socio-economic development, making life of the people in the state prosperous and happier.

Appendix

Central Places in Manipur : Functional Set-up and Centrality Score

Central Place	Population	Main Workers		Centrality Score
		Agricultural	Non-Agricultural	
1	2	3	4	5
Imphal	198535	1581	50207	39.50
Imphal East (Porompat)	58055	854	12493	23.56
Imphal East (Porompat)	58055	854	12493	23.56
Thongju	8296	516	1916	3.61
Kshetrigao	6872	470	1036	1.95
Heingang	4928	825	835	1.57
Koirengei	1325	43	86	0.16
Keirao Bitra	1697	311	307	0.58
Tulihal	3930	733	457	0.86
Andro	6797	1787	178	0.33
Changamdabi	3817	754	288	0.54
Moirang Purel	1266	441	71	0.13
Sawombung	2271	613	318	0.59
Lamlai	3606	928	279	0.53
Chingangbam	3575	421	855	1.61
Sagolmang	815	378	57	0.11
Khundrakpam	3960	897	651	1.23
Laikot	3561	1516	209	0.39
Imphal West (Lamphelpat)	140480	727	37714	50.91
Imphal West (Lamphelpat)	140480	727	37714	50.91
Iroisemba	3801	373	1001	1.35
Naoriya Pakhanglakpa	6032	101	1614	2.18

1	2	3	4	5
Lamsang	5635	1285	448	0.60
Sekmai	4288	947	494	0.67
Kanglatongbi	3648	1182	419	0.56
Khonghampat	2032	637	287	0.39
Phayeng	2071	653	129	0.17
Mayang Langjing	2136	755	179	0.24
Patsoi	3805	1434	226	0.31
Konthoujam	3025	892	350	0.47
Lamjaotongba	7340	239	1665	2.25
Maisnam Kangmong	3344	825	307	0.41
Maklang	1404	423	111	0.15
Wangoi	6764	1340	712	0.96
Mayang Imphal	16570	3964	1504	2.03
Lilong Chajing	9427	937	1709	2.31
Samurou	7757	1406	942	1.27
Monsangei	2373	91	762	1.03
Hiyangthang	3436	600	449	0.61
Kodompokpi	2242	620	345	0.46
Thoubal	33011	7021	3845	15.36
Thoubal	33011	7021	3845	15.36
Khongjom	1671	463	136	0.54
Heirok	1932	555	110	0.44
Yairipok	6911	1522	726	2.90
Sikhong Sekmai	5339	1378	625	2.02
Wangjing	5609	1430	505	2.01
Lilong	13822	2018	1414	5.65
Haoreibi	3083	463	288	1.15
Leisangthem	4314	1192	217	0.87
Moijing	4496	1093	614	2.45
Irong Chesaba	2878	667	14	0.06
Kakching	24437	6552	3020	12.06
Kakching Khunou	8234	2149	2789	11.14
Wabgai	6228	2043	550	2.20
Sugnu	4058	1215	388	1.55
Hiyanglam	5219	1679	437	1.71
Waikhong	1210	439	158	0.62
Pallel	3230	742	368	1.44
Bishnupur	8046	1253	1339	5.80

1	2	3	4	5
Bishnupur	8046	1253	1339	5.80
Nachou	3256	758	558	2.42
Ningthoukhong	9458	1675	1657	7.18
Ngaikhong Khullen	4675	1119	812	3.52
Phubala	2073	356	488	2.11
Keinou	3733	1145	365	1.58
Nambol	12630	2901	2074	8.98
Oinam	5307	1841	622	2.69
Utlou	2583	544	587	2.54
Leimapokpam	5803	1801	538	2.33
Irengbam	2587	763	240	1.04
Moirang	15443	3057	2439	10.57
Thanga	12386	1213	2807	12.16
Kwakta	5041	1392	364	1.58
Kumbi	7251	1946	585	2.53
Wangoo Ahallup	6460	2423	411	1.78
Saiton	5359	1568	355	1.54
Senapati	472	323	17	0.17
Tadubi	2099	847	190	1.91
Makhan Centre	1223	778	84	0.85
Punanamei	3045	1257	377	3.80
Mao Songsong	2623	1252	188	1.89
Tinsong	936	323	29	0.29
Yangkhullen	1637	1170	68	0.68
Maram Centre	836	346	38	0.38
Paomata	426	114	116	1.17
Tunggam Khullen	2833	1815	76	0.77
Liyai Khullen	3201	1134	68	0.68
Laii	1840	772	48	0.48
Purul	3346	1418	45	0.45
Oinam	2670	826	72	0.73
Phaibung Khullen	1601	719	25	0.25
Khongdei Khuman	633	279	8	0.08
Thingba Khunou	1308	771	24	0.24
Saikul	1192	114	116	1.17
Laikoiching	576	217	58	0.58
Thangal Surung	989	328	59	0.59
Leitanpokpi	546	227	28	0.28
Thankangphai	672	223	47	0.47

1	2	3	4	5
Phunam Maring	875	445	40	0.40
Kangpokpi	2830	606	497	4.99
Keithalmanbi	2936	759	265	2.67
Kalapahar	4939	1497	205	2.06
Chalwa	1484	625	24	0.24
Saitu	700	274	32	0.32
Motbung	2860	522	321	3.23
Leimakhong	596	10	75	0.76
Kangchup	224	76	29	0.29
Tamenglong	7733	361	59	1.26
Tousem	1181	526	32	0.68
Old Magulong	676	480	20	0.43
Thiulon	732	290	35	0.75
Oinamlong	958	259	25	0.53
Namtiram	415	140	22	0.47
Tamenglong	7733	361	59	1.26
Marangjing	1268	393	62	1.32
Akhui	828	418	50	1.06
Haochong	828	418	50	1.06
Shongphel Khunou	793	338	42	0.89
Awangkhul	1147	502	40	0.85
Tamei	1330	257	200	4.26
Langmei	759	183	27	0.57
Kadi	1444	781	22	0.47
Lenglong	871	273	21	0.45
Chaton	1134	540	14	0.30
Lenta	1028	474	9	0.19
Nungba	1245	410	136	2.90
Khoupum Chinthak	2996	1138	223	4.75
Noney	2230	721	207	4.41
Dolang	896	289	78	1.66
Lubanglong	665	213	47	1.00
Nungnang	1315	564	64	0.98
Churachandpur	33666	3917	5659	37.92
Parbung	2166	866	147	0.98
Senvon	2758	1403	67	0.45
Pherzawl	1342	547	044	0.29
Tinsuoung	823	411	31	0.14

1	2	3	4	5
Patpuimun	836	338	17	0.11
Tipaimukh (Sipuikon)	547	338	6	0.04
Sibapurikhal	561	225	23	0.15
Thanlon	2819	1022	221	1.48
Bukpi	1303	384	81	0,54
Mualnuam	1027	436	53	0.35
Suangsang	986	417	21	0.14
Leijangphai	505	216	8	0.05
Kaihlam	466	241	4	0.03
Henglep	513	114	24	0.16
Santing	1071	472	48	0.32
Charoi Khullen	518	113	19	0.11
Vungbuk	572	285	21	0.14
S. Nabil	623	542	12	0.08
Lhengjang	352	165	4	0.03
Samulamlan	118	25	8	0.05
Sagang	1277	361	215	1.44
Ngariyan	666	126	60	0.43
Keirap Khunthak	290	88	54	0.36
Khoirentak Khunou	364	65	42	0.28
Churachandpur	33666	3917	5659	37.92
Saikot	2337	314	312	2.09
Mata	1447	513	185	1.24
Thingkangphai	1685	515	182	1.22
Teiseng	1227	346	105	0.70
Lhangbung (Geljang)	946	304	96	0.64
Gangpimaul	877	106	143	0.96
Singngat	2969	944	206	1.38
Behiang	1195	357	69	0.46
Suvangdoh	893	372	34	0.23
Kangkap	954	414	30	0.20
Muallum	573	279	19	0.13
Lungching	627	442	16	0.11
Chandel	1558	179	481	6.76
Moreh	9673	1052	2251	31.65
Tengnoupal	621	200	66	0.93
Narum	293	131	25	0.36
Aimol Khullen	417	221	7	0.10
Leibi	416	255	7	0.10

1	2	3	4	5
Chalsom Tengnoupal	313	182	11	0.15
Machi	952	547	29	0.41
Lamlong Khullen	670	330	30	0.42
Tollen	418	146	36	0.51
Khoibu	361	109	25	0.36
Kangshang	322	167	8	0.11
Chandel	1558	179	481	6.76
Lambung (Phungchung)	622	184	93	1.31
Liwa Khullen	484	156	61	0.86
Khudei Khunou	532	33	47	0.52
Komlathabi	600	58	27	0.38
Larong Khunou	168	87	11	0.15
Tonsen Khullen	305	104	23	0.32
Chakpikarong	556	282	33	0.46
Khunbung Khunou	794	284	132	1.86
New Somtal	1001	474	90	1.26
Molcham	530	207	41	0.58
Sugnu Lamhang	560	156	50	0.70
Khongkang Sawompa	607	346	41	0.58
Haika	562	380	36	0.51
Ukhrul	10440	2318	1918	16.59
Chingai	892	336	58	0.50
Chingjaroi Christian	917	294	102	1.53
Paoyi	1556	515	78	0.67
Jessami	1365	530	75	0.64
Kharasom	942	405	75	0.64
New Tusom	937	202	48	0.41
Paorei	960	430	30	0.25
Ukhrul	10440	2318	1918	16.59
Hundung	4130	1211	607	5.34
Tolloi	2685	602	273	4.52
Tuinem	2474	646	305	2.88
Sanakeithal	1508	418	186	1.61
Khamasom	1542	609	137	1.18
Mapum	742	410	52	0.45
Kasom Khullen	620	209	55	0.47
Nambashi	300	101	32	0.27
Mawai	655	310	30	0.25
Khamlang	324	124	26	0.22

1	2	3	4	5
Nongdam	270	139	5	0.04
Kangkuk	222	91	5	0.04
Kamjong	903	270	133	1.15
Ningthi	730	210	127	1.09
Chatrik Khullen	946	369	117	1.01
Grihang	530	189	71	0.61
Maku	431	177	63	0.54
Nampisha	477	199	61	0.52
Chamu	413	156	49	0.43
Phungyar	565	138	134	1.16
Thawai	706	105	73	0.63
Sekibung	757	284	42	0.36
Lungphu	477	174	33	0.28
Chadong	634	210	28	0.24
Sorbung	429	162	17	0.16
Phalang	267	112	23	0.20
Jiribam	5969	335	1628	44.79
Jiribam	5969	335	1628	44.79
Hilghat	2006	187	266	7.32
Latingkhal	1276	242	102	2.00
Jakuradhor	1462	258	178	4.90
Sonapur	1415	461	68	1.87
Borobekra	644	98	114	3.13
Boroikhal	149	-	64	1.76

The centrality has been worked out on the basis of non-agricultural population of the central place multiplied by 100 and then divided by the non-agricultural population of the planning region-the hinterland of the growth centre.

Source : Census of India 1991.

Bibliography

Berry, B.J.L., 'A Note on Central Place Theory and the Range of a Good, *Economic Geography,* Vol. 34, 1958.

Bhat, L.S., *et al*, *Micro-Level Planning : A Case Study of Karnal area, Haryana, India*, K,B. Publication, New Delhi,1976.

Bhat, L.S., *Strategy for Integrated Area Development : Case Study of North Kanara District (Karnataka)*, Concept Publishing Company, New Delhi, 1988.

Boudville, J.R., *Problems of Regional Economic Planning*, University Press, Edinburgh, 1966.

Brown, R., *Statistical Account of the Native State of Manipur and the Hill Terriotry under its Rule*, Office of the Superintendent of Government Printing, Calcutta, 1873

Brush, John E. and H.E. Bracey, 'Rural Service Centres in South-Western Wisconsin and Southern England', in H. M. Mayer and C.F. Cohn (ed.), *Readings in Urban Geography*, University of Chicago, Chicago, 1967.

Census of India 1961, *District Census Handbook-Manipur* Government of Manipur, Imphal, 1964.

Census of India 1991, *Final Population Totals-Manipur State Primary Census Abstract* (1993); *General Population Tables-Manipur Part II-A* (1996), Directorate of Census Operations, Manipur, Imphal.

Census of India, *Regional Divisions of India-A Cartographic Analysis - Manipur,* Vol. 13, Series 1, Registrar General and Census Commissioner India, Government of India, New Delhi, 1988.

Champion, Harry G. and S.K. Seth, *The Forest Types of India*, Government of India, New Delhi, 1968

Chatterjee, S.P., 'Physiography', *The Gazetteer of India*, Vol. I, Ministry of Information and Broadcasting, Government of India, Delhi, 1965.

Christaller, Walter, *Die Zantralen Orte in Suddeutschland*, Gustav Fischer Verlag, Jena 1933, Baskin, C.W. (trans), *Central Places in Southern Germany*, Prentice Hall Inc., Englewood Cliffs, N.J., 1966.

Darwent, D.F., 'Growth Poles and Growth Centres in Regional Planning', *Environment and Planning*, Vol.1,1969.

Das, M.M. and L. Dutta, 'Regional Variation in Land Use and Agriculture in North-East India', *North-EasternGeographer*, Vol. 18, 1986.

Devi, H. Gitabali, Micro-Level Planning : A Case Study of Bishnupur District, Manipur, Ph. D. Thesis (unpublished), Manipur University, 1991.

Directorate of Economics and Statistics, *Economic Review 1994-95* (1998); *Meteorological Data of Manipur* 1972-82 (1983) and 1983-90 (1991); *Statistical Abstract of Manipur* 1998 (1999); *Tribal Bench Mark Survey 1983* (1985), Government of Manipur, Imphal.

Dun, E.W., *Gazetteer of Manipur*, Office of the Superintendent of Government Printing, Calcutta, 1886.

Evans, Geoffrey and Antony Brett-James, *Imphal- A Flower on Lofty Heights*, Macmillan and Co., London, 1960.

Forest Department, *Statistical Bulletin 1995-96*, Govt. of Manipur, Imphal, 1996.

Godlund, S., 'The Functions and Growth of Bus Traffic within the sphere of Urban Influence', *Land Studies Geography Series B, Human Geography*, No.18,1956.

Government of Manipur, *Eighth Five Year Plan 1992-97*, Vol. I (1992) ; *Sixteenth Quinquennial Census of Livestock 1997* (1998), *Manipur Gazatte* No. 382 (1994) and No. 104 (1997), Imphal.

Hagget, Peter, *Geography A Modern Synthesis*, Harper & Row, New York, 1979

Hansen, N.M. (ed.), *Regional Economic Development*, The Free Press, New York, 1972.

Jefferson, M., 'Distribution of the World City Folks', *Geographical Review*, Vol. 21, 1931.

Johnson, E.A.J., *The Organisation of Space in Developing Countries*, Harvard University Press, Cambridge, Mass., 1970.

Joshi, S.C. (ed.), *Rural Development in the Himalaya : Problems and Prospects*, Gyanodaya Prakashan, Nainital, 1984.

Khan, Wahiduddin and K.S. Ramesh, *Integrated Area Development Plan for West District, Manipur*, National Institute of Community Development, Hyderabad, 1976.

Khan, Wahiduddin and R.N. Tripathy, *Plan for Integrated Rural Development in Pauri Garhwal*, National Institute of Community Development, Hyderabad, 1976.

Kuklinski, A. (ed.), *Growth Poles and Growth Centres in Regionl Planning,* Mouton, Paris, 1972.

Lasuen, J.R., 'On Growth Poles', *Urban Studies*, Vol.6, 1979

Losch, August, *The Economics of Location*, Yale University Press, New Haven, 1954.

Misra, G.K., Jatin De and J.S. Sodhi, *Block Level Planning with Focus on Employment Generation*, Rawat Publications, Jaipur, 1987.

Misra, R.P., K.V. Sundaram and V.L.S. Prakasa Rao, *Regional Devleopment Planning in India-A New Strategy*,Vikas Publishing House, New Delhi, 1974.

National Council of Applied Economic Research (NCAER), *Techno-Economic Survey of Manipur-Economic Report,* Manipur Administration, Imphal, 1961.

National Remote Sensing Agency (NRSA), *Report on Land Use/Land Cover-Manipur State 1988-89*, Directorate of Science, Technology and Environment, Government of Manipur, Imphal, 1990.

North Eastern Council, *Basic Statistics of North-Eastern Region 1995*, North Eastern Council Secretariat, Shillong, 1995.

Perroux, Francois, 'Note sur la Notion de Pole croissance', *Economic Applique*, January-June 1955.

Planning Commission, Government of India, *First Five Year Plan* (1952); *Second Five Year Plan* (1956); *Third Five Year Plan* (1961); *Fourth Five Year Plan* (1969); *Fifth Five Year Plan* (1974) ; *Sixth Five Year Plan (*1980) ; *Seventh Five Year Plan* (1978), Manager of Publications, Delhi.

Planning Department, Mid-term Appraisal for the Ninth Five year Plan 1997-2002, Government of Manipur, Imphal, 1999.

Reilly, William J., *The Law of Retail Gravitation*, Knickerbocker Press, New York, 1931.

Rushton, G., 'Planning Practices in the context of Location Theories', in Lalit K. Sen (ed.), *Readings on Micro-level Planning and Rural Growth Centres*, National Institute of Community Development, Hyderabad, 1972.

Sanjenbam, Vedaja, 'Floods and Flood Control Measures in Manipur', *Himalaya-Man and Nature*, Vol. 15, 1991.

Sen, Lalit K., *et al*, *Growth Centres in Raichur : An Integrated Area Development Plan for a District in Karnataka*, National Institute of Community Development, Hyderabad, 1975.

Sen, Lalit K., *et al, Planning Rural Growth Centres for Integrated Area Development : A Study in Miryalguda Taluka*, National Institute of Community Development, Hyderabad, 1971.

Singh, H.P., *Resource Appraisal and Planning in India : A Case Study of a Backward Region,* Rajesh Publications, New Delhi, 1979.

Singh, Jagdish, *Central Places and Spatial Organisation in a Backward Economy : Gorakhpur Region-A Study in Integrated Regional Development,* Uttar Bharat Bhoogol Parishad, Gorakhpur, 1979.

Singh, Kanchan, Regional Development and Planning in a Backward Region : A Case Study of District Banda (Unpublished Project Report), Indian Council of Social Science Research, New Delhi,1989.

Singh, Kashi N., 'Spatial Patterns of Central Places in the Middle Ganga Valley, India', *National Geographical Journal of India*, Vol. 12, 1966.

Singh, R.P., *Geography of Manipur*, National Book Trust, India, New Delhi, 1982.

Singh, R.P., 'Spatial Planning in Chandel District, Manipur', *North Eastern Gegorapher*, Vol 17, 1985.

Singh, R.P. and Vedaja Sanjenbam, 'Rural Development and Micro-level Planning : A Case Study of Jiribam Block, Manipur', *North Eastern Geographer*, Vol.23 1991.

Singh, Surendra, *Integrated Area Development and Planning*, Shree Publishing House, New Delhi, 1990.

Singh, Th. Munindro, 'District-wise Development Profile in Manipur' (unpublished paper), Planning Department, Government of Manipur, Imphal 1993.

Tripathy, R.N., *et al, Block Plan in the District Frame : A Development Plan for Madakasira Block in Ananthapur District, Andhra Pradesh*, National Institute of Rural Development, Hyderabad, 1980.

Tripathy, R.N., *et al, Planning for Integrated Rural Development Programme-Amalapuram Block (East Godavari District , A.P)*, National Institute of Rural Development, Hyderabad, 1981.

Ullman, Edward L., ' A Theory of Location for Cities', *American Journal of Sociology*, Vol.46, 1941.

Von Thunen, Johanan H., *Der isolierte Staat in Beziehung auf Landwirtschft una Nationalokonomic,* Rostock, 1826, Wartenburgh, C.M. (trans.) *Von Thunen's Isolated State*, Oxford University Press, London, 1966.

Wanmali, Sudhir, *Regional Planning for Social Facilites- An Examination of Central Place Concepts and their Application : A Case Study of Eastern Maharashtra*, National Institute of Community Development, Hyderabad, 1973.

Index

1. The Khamba - Thoibi Dance

2. Pung Cholom

3. Radha Krishna Dance

4. Tribal Dance of Manipur

5. Loktak Lake

6. Govinda Ji Temple

7. Netaji Subash Chandra Bose

8. Bro-antler Deer (Sangai)

9. Bishnu Mandir

10. Chorus Museum

11. Floating House

12. Kangla Fort

13. Manipuri Dance

14. Manipuri Dance